The Girl Can't Help It:

Love, Loss, &

What I Drank

jenburger

DEDICATION

To the man who helped me get to my level.

He knows who he is.

CONTENTS

The Girl Can't Help It: Love, Loss, & What I Drank

ACKNOWLEDGMENTS

Thanks to my Dad for unconditionally supporting me. My words cannot express how much I appreciate you.

My kiddos, you are growing up to be amazing ladies, and I'm so excited to see where you go in life.

Special thanks to Marquez aka Burrito, who gave me the nickname Jenburger, and is one of my cover models LOL

To Katie, Dawni, Courtney and Antoine, Josiah (Jaby!), My very good (and twin!) friend Ms. Chocolate Thai , Superbetch, James at Arkain Music, Nicole (Rubes!), Shannon, Carrie, Tish, Nikki, the other Nicole (Cocomele!) Salvatore Jenkins, Aleek, Jessie, and Laryssa at www.commansentence.com!

Also, special thanks to those who always support me in general, no matter what crazy shit I'm doing …Denise Groseclose (and Dave, Cassi, and Carl…you all are the best!), Kuddie, Philly, Mr. DNA Cowboy, Rudy, and LaundryMatt. Donel & Shannon, Elene, and the whole family at Donel's Espresso and The Spunky Monkey (Byron, Doreen and Art, and Joel—thanks for listening to all my stories and laughing at me), Sophia (I miss you!), Charyn, Q-Dot, Drew, Paul PC!, Eden, Miss Mia *Cupcake*, Sparkly miss Shonda, DJ Peg, Mr. Jay Barz, My PIC Angie, Jaki, and a big thanks to Miss Tasha Dionne.

And to every man who screwed up, a special thanks.
I wrote a book about your asses.

Xoxo,
jen, jenburger, jburgs, j, the hussy

The Girl Can't Help It: Love, Loss, & What I Drank

OPEN LETTERS

10 Ways to NOT Be a Ho

Dear Ladies (and the rest of you females)

The more I read, the more people I come across, and the more messes I clean up after tramp-ass women, the more I feel the need to write this long overdue blog.

So, here it is in all its glory.

Ladies, sexuality is a power, and it is a power to be respected. It's also a double edged sword. And just as quickly as you can use sexuality to your benefit, you can get sex involved and the power slips right through your hands and will be used against you.

I wear sexy clothes. I sport cleavage. And curves. And skirts that showcase my ass. But I hold my head high in every room I walk into. The money I buy things with is mine, and it wasn't handed to me at the price of my dignity. And when I'm in a relationship, I can walk into any room with my man and he's proud to say I'm his girl.

So here's my advice.

10 Ways to NOT Be A Ho

1. Don't Have Sex in Circles.

This is my Numero UNO.

What do I mean? Don't have sex with a dude. And then his friend. Or his friend's friend. Or his boss, coworker, favorite bartender, neighbor, classmate, producer, brother, business contact...I could go on, but unless you're incredibly dumb, you get what I'm saying. And if you ARE dumb, you're likely going to be a slut anyway.

I don't sleep around in circles, and sometimes this means I don't hook up with a man I really *really* want. But guess what? I hold my head high in any room, and I've never embarrassed any of my men by standing next to him in a room full of men that have smashed. There's billions of men in the world. No one cares about your sob story of how you liked them all for different reasons.

2. Don't Kiss and Tell

The masses don't really care about specific details of your sexual activities, or how long you did it in any specific position. Sure, some men may talk about that amongst themselves, but we aren't men. And additionally, even if they've talked about it a thousand times with their friends, they do not want to talk about their wife or girlfriend like that. Just the jumpoffs.

3. If You're A Mother, ACT LIKE IT.

Remember all the jokes kids tell each other, like "Your momma is suuuuuuuuuch a ho…."? Don't be THAT bitch. I was a young mom, and I do silly things like party with my friends on my birthday and wear my Catwoman mask around the city. But I never showed off anything my family would be embarrassed of, nor did I end up flashing my tits to a crowd or send naked pics out to mass quantities of recipients.
There is a fine line between young and wild and just skanky.
Find that line and don't cross it.

4. Don't Be A Sloppy Bitch

I mean this in so many different senses of the words.

Take care of yourself. Present yourself like a lady. Don't have your gut spilling over your jeans. Don't have your ass crack hanging out. Don't wear completely sheer shirts, shorts that give you camel toe, or skirts that let half of your ass cheeks stick out. Unless you're a stripper or prostitute. Yes, you'll get lots and lots of looks, but don't be surprised when you get no respect.

5. Don't Have Sex With Strangers

Who are you about to let inside? Do you know their name? Their last name? Any of their friends? Anything about what kind of person they are? What they do for a living? If not, they must not know those things about you....do you not love yourself enough to find out?

6. Don't Have Sex "For" Things

Don't have sex for a job, a promotion, fame, recognition, to get free stuff, or to have a place to stay. Don't have sex to keep a relationship because you're taken care of.

Don't have sex with your boss, business associates, etc. Let me just say this: you'll never be a credible businesswoman if you're sitting in negotiations somewhere and they're staring at you remembering when your legs were wrapped up behind your head.

And, when other women in business find out, they'll resent you for being the reason we all get treated like sleeping with someone is a requirement to make a deal go through.

If you want to be a prostitute, just do it the real way. Don't be a coward.

7. Don't Let Anyone Disrespect You

Unless you deserve it. Don't let someone demand something

of you. Or tell you what they want without asking you. Don't let someone take pictures when you don't want them taken. Don't let someone treat you like a second-class citizen. Don't let someone disrespect you in public, act like you're stupid or worthless, or call you out of name. If they do, LEAVE. Don't make excuses or cry or let it get to you. Just move on, and don't look back.

8. Don't Do Naked Pics or Sextapes

Unless you want to see them online. Here's the thing, I won't even tell you ''unless you really trust'' anyone. Ever. Because usually when we trust, we do it too young or too soon. Now I realize we're grown and may wish to do this...If you DO send pics, send them without your face in them. And even then, be careful.

Do you have a tattoo that identifies you? I ask this because you don't know what the future holds for you. And nothing would suck more than to get married to someone and he has to see a video of his wife having sex with other people. I can't help but think of famous people whose relationships have been ruined by these. I bet many of them regret those videos today.

9. Don't Ever (Ever) Have Sex With A Man Who Is Married/In A Relationship

Just don't. This has nothing to do with him and everything to do with you. Don't be THAT bitch. He will find someone else to have sex with outside his commitment. And it has nothing to do with you. But never be "the other woman". And even more important, never ever ever (ever) get with a friend's man. In fact, even your friend's ex is off limits. PERIOD. (This is the same as number one, but on the flip side).

Listen, these men that cheat on their wives/girlfriends will tell you everything you need to hear to think they'll leave or feel bad for their situation. They'll say how bad it is, or run to you when the woman they're committed to isn't the very best to them. And then they'll stay with her. They'll keep sleeping with her, sleeping with you, and often times, sleeping with anyone and everyone else around.

Don't let them put you in that position. Screw them, and their wayward dick. (Actually, *don't* screw them.)

10. Don't Have Sex More Than One Person At A Time

Don't juggle several sexual partners at once. I'm not even going to explain this one. I think it's obvious that having a bunch of dicks coming at you regularly is just skeevy in general. And YOU look dumb for it.

Dear Men,

If I don't explicitly,

specifically, directly

request a picture of your veiny, erect

penis,

(and trust me…I won't)

please don't send me one.

That is all

xoxo,

Jen

The "Do's and Don'ts of The Friend Zone"

Dear Everyone,

After a recent (horrible) experience involving a mutinous person living in my "Friend Zone", I'd like to pause and direct your attention to the following Public Service Announcement.

If you are relocating a member of your "Dating Pool" to your "Friend Zone":

Do:

Communicate honestly. Always. Pay attention to signs that your occupant may be trying to scam a place in your Dating Pool. Deport the silly ass of anyone attempting to stage a coup and overthrow your government. Your Dating Pool and Friend Zone are not a democracy. That shit is an autocracy, and you're the dictator. Remember that.

Do NOT:

Discuss any potential for a transfer out of the Friend Zone if you don't mean that shit, because if the conversation is discussed by either party, the individual in the Friend Zone is likely going to start packing and prepare for the move. Also, never EVER ignore signs that the occupant is trying to relocate to your Dating Pool.

If you see these signs, and are not wishing to provide a warm welcome to the person, get that shit in check. Don't be coy. It only serves as the foundation for a big problem later.

If you have been/are being relocated to someone's Friend Zone:

Do:

Communicate honestly. Always. Also, accurately assess your ability to be a successful citizen. Assume that you are not special, and that staging a coup will result in severe battle wounds, followed
by epic failure, and is not worth the effort. Additionally, remember that you can relinquish your citizenship at any time,
and find another place to go. Leaving or staying is entirely your choice. Lastly, accept the rules established by the leader.
Accept the terms as is.

Do NOT:

Accept residency if you don't agree to the country's bylaws. Also, never ever (ever) try to overthrow the government. Ever. Don't think you'll 'convince' the person that they're in love with you....in fact, anyone shaking your head in disagreement right now, consider this:
the person assigning you to the friend zone has said that's where they are placing you. If, by chance, they're secretly wanting you in the dating pool (or worse...hoping you'll stage a coup), and they don't

fess up to that shit, you're in the middle of their game. "Game" is a polite dating term for "manipulation". "Manipulation" is a fancy five-syllable synonym for "lie". Are you pickin up what I'm gettin at? You're fancying a liar. Now, you're smarter than that, aren't you??

I'd like to acknowledge that it is perfectly normal to, over time, begin to wonder about people that have been in one zone or the other for too long..."maybe he/she and I could be great together" or "maybe he/she is better as my friend"...

Just know that crushy feelings happen, and as long as you keep them in check and disclose them as applicable (hey.....don't be scared. If you have a healthy relationship, open, honest discussion is just that-- discussion), then everyone's on the same page. Also, sometimes when you're dating someone, the passion might be lacking, and you might find yourself evaluating their residency in your Dating Pool. Again, be honest. You might find that they feel the same way.

Lastly, I stress, again, that anyone intentionally staging a coup in your Dating Pool or Friend Zone should be immediately treated as a treasonous bastard. You don't have time for that shit.

How do I know all this? I recently had a resident of my friend zone stage a battle and attempt to overthrow my government. And it really, really sucked. So heads up, everyone. Hope this helps.

Yep. That about covers it.

Dear Everyone Born Between 1970 and 1990,

Let's take a moment to address an issue that seems to be plaguing my generation. I try to stay gender-neutral as much as possible, but I direct this towards the ladies.

If you're going to do something, go hard or go home.

I'm talkin about gold digging.

Now I'll state, for the record, I think gold diggers are just a disgrace. I don't mean women who genuinely fall in love with ballers for who they are (all five of you), I mean you ladies who seek out the lifestyle and not the love.

I know a girl who seeks out the baller- types and will change everything she is to mold what he's looking for until she catches his ass. It seems every relationship she had was a man with money who took her (and her son) in (she, of course, has no apartment of her own) and she instantly upgrades her lifestyle. She is the queen of manipulation and best of all, will deny that shit to the end.

Most recently, she found a guy who she moved in with (slowly bringing her things over and bitching about her roommate until he gave in), ousting his other roommate.

He is an old-fashioned kinda guy. She brags about how he wants his wife to stay home and take care of the kids some day, being fully provided for.

She quickly (of course) became pregnant (her son is nine...and she's been having sex for the last nine years, but now suddenly had an 'accident'). To her surprise, he said he wasn't ready for a baby with her, and wanted to wait to get married.

She called me, asking me to take her to a clinic. In our discussion, she mentioned that "now he'll *really* have to pay", because it's going to take her "a *long* time to get over this". Meaning: she'll smother him in guilt and milk it for all its worth.

And she did. She quickly was bragging about all "their" new furniture (he bought it...she works part time for $12 an hour, he is a baller).

When I called her out, she denied it. We now are no longer friends.

I hate when women do this shit, because those of us who pride ourselves in *havin our own* carry "Baller Guilt". We won't have a man pay for *shyit* because we feel like we're pulling their bitch moves.

This is the same for child support.
Look, I raise kids, I know it's not cheap. I assume *some famous peoples'* kids need private school, security, etc. but I do *not* feel those children cost as much to raise as some of these women get.

In fact, let's say the mothers wants them to have the best of the best...I'm with that. She should work hard and earn the means to provide it for them.

And I see people on twitter asking what ever happened to the sacred union of marriage.

These broads. That's what happened. Ladies, get your own. I'd rather be half of an empire than a sponge.

 I don't blame you for being cautious of women's motives. And men who are working hard to pay the bills and barely makin it, I salute you. If you've been passed up for another man based on his bank account, she wasn't worth it anyway. I promise.

Ladies, if you're dating a man and you're a boss in your own right, here's a tip I got last year from a friend when my "Baller Guilt" had me ready to stop seeing someone:

"Take a few moments to really think about your man. Imagine him, his smile, and his presence. Now imagine him standing at the door ready for work in a polo shirt. Look close. There's a Burger King Logo. If you still want to hug him and would eat end-of-shift Whoppers with him
every night, he's a keeper.

Dear Men,

Now I'm sure you have plenty of women in your life who are telling you what they want, need, what you're doing wrong, etc. etc.

I'm gonna be real. I'm about to do the same.

Stay with me....

I'm gonna be brief and honest. I'm gonna say some things that may not apply to you, and other things you don't wanna
hear.

The good news?

I'll address the ladies next.

So if you would be so kind as to be patient, we'll get through this together.

Deal? Sweet. Let"s do this.

It's my understanding that the biggest problem ladies have is in the communication department. Which is no surprise. We talk. And talk and talk and talk. And you try your best to stay focused on everything we talk about.
But how about, and I only am suggesting this, you say "Baby, I'm so busy with work right now" or "Can I call/text/talk to you after I'm

done with ____" (and then you actually call).

In fact, how about you beat her to the talking in the first place??

Shoot out a good morning text and say you'll talk to her later. Tell her to have an amazing day. You know what she'll do? Be happy all damn day and you don't get all the texts or calls.

I also know it's hard to open up and be honest, but just try it. Tell the ones you like that you like them, and with ones you don't like, just *don't say anything*. Don't throw out tiny things that they can get false hopes from. Keep it biz but
friendly. Not so hard is it?

Another thing that makes us (yeah, I'll keep it 100) go weirdo on you is to be kept in limbo while you figure something out/play the hot and cold game. If you aren't sure, *say* so! If you need time to yourself, speak on it. And if you regret opening up and getting all close at some point, just ask for a day or two to sort things out. I assure you, not asking means we assume the worst, and that's when we go weirdo. Some girls will cry and text and freak out, some will find the comfort of another guy, and some (me, for example) will write your ass off. And then where are you? You're somewhere thinking we didn't care and that we're a bitch.

#AmIRight?

I also will say this: if you're done with a relationship, end it!

Don't stir shit up to instigate fights, don't look for flaws in us and point them out (even though we all know when love is gone, all the other party's flaws seem to amplify), and stop waiting for "the" fight to end it all, and #forfuckssake don't *cheat*! Just do it. Now.

We all know you dudes like to be right all the time, as do we. And while I may be a traitor right now, I'm just going to say it….shouldn't you just be right this time?

Give her nothing shitty to say about you. Even leaving is a favor, and explain it like that. Say that your feelings have changed rather than treat her poorly.

Do you know what will happen? Really, most will try to talk you into staying. But, sticking to your guns and leaving, she'll talk you up and all her friends will put you on some "ex- boyfriend" pedestal. You'll never be embarrassed to run into her, and she'll always secretly pine for you.

See? You're already getting an ego boost.

So do it the right way. You never know when you'll meet a super bad one and your reputation will have preceded you. Don't you want her to hear nothing but good press? I thought so.

You're welcome.

PALATE CLEANSER

"When the King shows up, I will kiss his ring, but I have nothing to offer the court jesters".

My very good friend texted me this a while back and it was so good, I saved it. It cracked me up. It rings true for both men and women, because we all know both can be less than the best.

I talked with some friends about the act of overinvesting and how sometimes we end up upset with a poor return on the investment. You win some, you lose some, but when it comes to your kingdom, weigh your decisions carefully, and never compromise your standards.

jenburger

FUCKERY

Revolving Doors

Remember being a kid in the summertime, playing outside, getting up off the slip-n- slide and running in the house to get some toys, Kool-aid, or to refill your squirt gun?

And remember your mom or grandma getting pissed because you were tracking dirt inside or leaving sloppy wet foot prints all over the kitchen floor?

Kid shit is the best, but there's a time when everyone needs to grow up.

I have a friend who took back her kid's dad after being MIA for 72 hours and coming home with the name "Stacy" tattooed on his arm. Her name was Claire.

I have a friend who bought his fiancé a car after taking her back when he learned she had cheated on him with four men. Two months later, he came home to an empty apartment, no car, and half his bank account empty. She left with his best friend.

My point is, we seem to override complete deal-breakers when we love someone, and we really need to find the difference between "you fucked up" and "you publicly humiliated me/physically endangered me/fucked up my life". I'm all about working past issues when you love someone, because that's the beauty of unconditional love.

But "unconditional love" only exists when both sides participate. Otherwise it's a doormat loving an unapologetic asshole.

Revolving doors are great for hotels and department stores, and that's about it. If you have someone who is like a little kid in the summertime, I highly encourage you to do like my mom did, and finally stand at the door, block it, and say "In or out. Pick *one*." Before they track dirt all over your house and leave a big water mess all over your kitchen floor.

Brand Recognition: The Heartbreaker

Take a moment with me, and let's talk marketing. Stay with me. I assure you this relates to love.

Let's go on a test drive of a new car. Walk up and see how deep and rich the color of the paint is. The clear coat is fresh, and the curves of the car are defined and even highlighted by the new paint.

Slide your hand along the handle of the driver's side door and open it up. The smell of new car wraps itself around you and begs for you to take a seat.

As you sit, you feel the soft, supple leather caress your body. Slide your hands on the steering wheel. You wanna take this shit for a spin.

Now, the salesman starts his pitch:

"Yeah, this thing will do zero to sixty in five seconds. It gets 30 miles per gallon and has a deluxe racing package.

On the other hand, you should know some facts about the car. It has been in several accidents; it did run over and kill a man. It also won't start quite often, so you'll be shit out of luck if you're trying to get anywhere.

It may or may not make you sick, as it's had lots of dirty drivers before you and it hasn't been sanitized, just detailed.

Oh yeah, and the interest rate on the financing is shit, and you'll be paying a lot to maintain it, since it has no warranty.

But despite all the danger, unreliability, and cost, it's gonna look soooooo great in your driveway!

Do we have a deal??"

I hope you're completely turned off by this right now.

Why?

Because men and women do this all the time in relationships. They tell you *exactly* who they are, and expect you to sign up. Most of the time, they're almost
proud of it.

I'm great at recognizing jerks. Typically, I easily spot them because, just like a familiar logo, I see the "Made in the Land of Assholishness" tag.

Talking with a friend last night about Taio Cruz's song "Break Your Heart", I realized how often we all over look the blatant advertising of others.

I am not one to hide the fact that I have commitment issues. I don't disguise it or sugarcoat it, and, most importantly, I'm working on it. I don't find it to be my favorite character trait, nor have I ever, at any time, bragged about it to a man.

This song makes me crazy because it throws out the following message:

"I'm pretty much premeditating to do some mean, cold hearted shit to you, love you and leave you, and then nonchalantly move onto the next to repeat this process. In the end, I will continue to solidify my title as a heartbreaker."

I'm bothered not by his honesty, but by the fact that he's committing premeditated fuckery.

Coming from the side guilty of what I'll call "Accidental Assholishness", I know sometimes you don't mean to be harmful, it just happens. And you don't wear a badge of honor from it; you wear what is more like an orange safety vest, warning others to be cautious of what's ahead.

When my friends meet this kinds of guys (and girls!!!), I'm always so frustrated that they keep talking to/dating/having sex with these assholes. Why? What on earth would make you sign that kind of contract??

It's one thing to have someone who is working on becoming a better person/lover/friend/boyfriend/girlfriend.

It's something completely different for someone to unapologetically announce their premeditated fuckery and expect you to be on board.

Take what they say at face value and decide if you want what is being placed before you. And don't dabble in "what if's" or

take on a fixer-upper if it doesn't seem ready and stable enough be fixed.

Maya Angelou once said, "The first time someone shows you who they are, believe them."

Didja hear that?? *Believe them.*

Is No Relationship the New Relationship??

Ladies and gentlemen, I'm seeing a trend. I'm seeing a trend of people having a boo, but owing nothing to anyone. I've got a handful of girlfriends doing this. What cracks me up is my guy friends are doing it too, but they call it "Fucking".

A discussion with the guys at the table last night turned into a discussion about what men do when they're truly interested in a woman. It does not involve letting her get down with other dudes. Period.

Ladies, you can play the "independent" card all you like, but I'm not buying it. No matter what, one side in this situation is always wanting more or it would be called "fucking" or "friends with benefits", not an "open relationship".

Men are territorial, and ladies, keep it real: you are just as protective of the man you like.

I'm selective about who I give any part of myself. Very selective. That means I won't bullshit people, I won't give energy.

I don't genuinely want to give, and, most importantly, I can't give bits and pieces to several different people.

I'm in or out. It's that simple.
That said, I can flirt like crazy, enjoy the company (without putting my

legs in the air) of many men, and entertain the thought of taking things to the next level when I'm single. But if I'm regularly giving all my energy to, sleeping with, and allowing a man to become a major factor in my life, I'm just incapable of turning and choosing another man, or five, to give little pieces of me to.

Ladies and gentlemen, don't kid yourselves. Whichever side suggests keeping things light, casual, "open", etc. is either A)a player with a heart (aka, not one to cheat/commit fuckery, but is still making slapping sounds with other people) or B)Keeping you in play until someone "better" comes around, at which point you will go from "I just wanna keep this light" to "I feel we've grown apart".

I promise you.

The Do's and Don'ts of Stalking

Actually, this list is an easy one. There are no "do's" of stalking. And there's only one "don't".

Don't stalk anyone. At all. Ever. According to Wikipedia:

> "Stalking is a term commonly used to refer to unwanted attention by individuals (and sometimes groups of people) to others."

First, let's all agree that a boyfriend/girlfriend can't "stalk" you. They can be jealous, possessive, and just plain fucking smothery, but that does not make them a stalker.

You can tell you're a stalker by the lack of reciprocation from the person you are "showering with attention". If you send texts that say "Hey gorgeous" and receive "Hi." or better yet, nothing, you need to proceed with caution. After a few (I'm gonna say three), you need to just fucking stop.

If you're sending a text and not receiving a response, so you follow with another. And a third "just in case", *just fucking stop.*

If you're staring at your crush's Twitter or Facebook page and clicking the links of people they're communicating with to see what they're saying and then studying that person *just fucking stop.*

If you're researching information on your crush and then memorizing the shit like it's about to appear on a licensing exam next week or interjecting it in conversation *just fucking stop.*

If you're watching their Twitter page to see where they're going Friday so you can "coincidentally" show up, *just fucking stop.*

For that matter, if you're coordinating, planning, or plotting *anything* so it can become a "coincidence", *just fucking stop.*

Going to an ex's favorite bar so you can see their new current? *Stoppit.*

Doing "drive by's"? *Stoppit.*

I could go on, and trust me, I've been the victim of people's severely stalkeriffic weirdo shit that goes far beyond anything listed above (once a guy got in with my parents at our family's restaurant and asked them if he could attend the family Christmas Eve because he was trying to date me...I know...
what in the motherfucking shit is that?!?!) I won't go on, because it's easy to check yourself by remembering that *anything not reciprocated is stalking.* Period.

Trying to push your way into someone else's heart, love life, family life, personal life, or apartment community is simply unacceptable.

I know, you think you've found someone wonderful, and that's great. But it is important that you remember that people don't see you as "persistent". They see you as a guy who may have a human skin suit at home and a girl in a well in your basement trying to entice your poodle, Precious, to the edge of the well with a chicken bone.

I promise you.

So, if you find yourself a bit "excited" about the amazing guy or girl you've found and you want to reel them in, I encourage you to remember that fish never swim up to a fisherman who's full speed ahead in his fishing boat chasing them. They swim up to the quiet, relaxed fisherman sitting on the dock throwing out the best bait and waiting.

And by "bait" I don't mean "roofies". Just so we're clear.

Rules of Engagement

Everyone has their ground rules, but sometimes they need to be put out there for others to see. I really sat and evaluated mine, and despite high standards for others in regards to honesty and attitude, my ground rules are pretty basic.

Here's my list. Pretty easy.

1. Don't fucking stalk me. EVER.

2. After three texts or phone calls to which I don't respond, just go away.

3. Please don't be the girl in the relationship, because that's my job.

4. Honesty. Always. And if there's anything else, please re-read number two. You're gonna need it.

5. Please share Fruity Pebbles with me. And never make me pour out that crumb shit at the bottom of the box when I try to make a bowl because you were too lazy to toss the box out. In exchange, I offer you control of the remote.

What does your list look like? If you don't know and you're

wondering why you're single and/or keep meeting the ''wrong ones'', this is a great starting point to refocus.

The Neverending Story

In response to an email, "how do you know if a guy is playing you?"
I offer this:

After a number of texts from an ex the other night, I had to just
put my phone away.

It was the texts you don't want to get, especially from the ex you care
for, but don't want. The texts that say they're waiting for you and that
you were the one meant for them.

It makes me wonder if so many of these people only want me or
hundreds...even thousands of other girls... because they're hard to get.

There's that element of chase in most men. It's what lights the fire
of excitement and intrigues them. It's what makes a woman ribbon
through his thoughts and take over his mind. It's the animalistic
thrill of the chase.

And, in some cases, they chase, catch, and that's that. They found one
(or the one) they want. There's other men, for whom it's all about the
chase. (Some women are this way, too...I've been that girl several
times...I like challenges).

Ladies (and men, for the women who do this), pay attention. Like
Steve Harvey says, "Command, not demand, respect". In other
words, be worthy of it and never ask it. It's there or it's not.

And never, ever, fall for the people who aren't willing to step up to the plate and give you what you deserve.

Ten tips to see someone is playing/trying to play you:

1. They want the bragging rights. They want to show you off to people. Or, early in the game, you have third parties hearing about them bragging about hanging with you, often times over exaggerating.

2. They take from you. In any way. They don't reach for the wallet, let you pay when they shouldn't, ask for benefits of the things you have (your job, your hookups, your friends, etc.).

3. They play the convenience game. They want you. When it's convenient. They call. When it's convenient. They're there. When it's convenient. And when it's not, well, you know.

4. There's just "something" weird. You know what I mean. Weird changes. Sometimes they're just not themselves. They're really nice, then a complete asshole. Then nice again. Never addressing the behavior. I don't mean moody. I mean...well, weird.

5. They're hot then cold. They want your time. Then show no interest. Then they're all flirty and "chasing" you. Then over it. You know this is the case when they're pursuing the shit out of you, then you don't hear from them, see them out with some other chick, then

the next day it's "Hey, baby" on a text. GTFOH.

6. Mind Fucking. This is much different, and far less enjoyable than regular fucking. This is weird twisted games with words. Script flipping. Mind fucking in general is a motherfuckingtittysuckingbullshitass thing. And it should never be permitted.

7. Fuckery. This should be self explanatory. But any kind of fuckery that is caught. He flirts with your friend then shrugs it off. She pulls some deceitful shit and lies to you.

8. Secrecy. Opposite of being bragadocious, there's the ones who want you to be too secret. They want you to be off their social networking pages, don't want to go in public (and you're not circus fat/don't have The Elephant Man's face). If he doesn't want to tell the world (or at least a good friend) about you, you're getting fucked. Literally and figuratively.

9. Disrespect. In general. Calling you out of name (men AND ladies). Anyone who cares for you isn't going to talk to you disrespectfully.

10. Blunt Playing. There are a very select group of people who can't see playing even right in front of their face. I've seen girls go out with a guy and he literally has another date there in the room and she's oblivious. "I think that's just his friend?". GTFOH. Both of you.

(S)He Who Laughs, Lasts

While doing reports today, the tv was on (because I hate to be alone in the quiet) and by some weird twist of fate, I looked up to see the face of a woman I recognized.

There on the "Lie Detector Test" show of one of the daytime tv talk shows, was "C" as we'll call her, talking about her love triangle situation.

"C" used to be my customer when I bartended, and she seemed to be pretty sweet and straight up. She did have a big beef with some girl we'll call "T", and I recall breaking up a pretty good fight between the two. The problem continued over several months, and I finally kicked "T" out of the bar because that beezy was always in some shyit. With "C", with a bunch of others...she just was always in the middle of something, always was crying, running off, etc.

#ComeOnDaughter

Anyway, as the show continues, out comes "T". They yell and "C" tries to slap the shit out of "T" because they both live with "E" (who is currently C's boyfriend but T's babys dad).

Still with me?

I watch all this happen, and the whole time, all I can think is this:

Why in the fuuuuuck is C even using energy towards this situation??

She seems like a decent person, she never had done anything shitty to people, and even apologized to me after she fought T, just because it disrespected my bar. Watching women fight for men who won't treat them right (or vice versa...I've seen men get treated like garbage by women, be publicly humiliated, and still come back for more) just breaks my heart.

When E and T failed the lie detector test, immediately there was the customary throwing of chairs, screaming, crying, and "Whyyyyyyyyyyyyy?". I wanted to jump into the television, pull C aside, and say "SHHHH. Look at both of these people. What in the world would you let them continue to steal your energy for?".

I've seen girls yank out chunks of each others' hair and leave them all over my bar because a man played them both. I've seen men break each other's noses over a complete slut. And I'm always astounded that they will take this frustration out on the third party, then focus so much energy on the person who cared so little, they threw the persons heart in a blender and hit "puree".

Once, I dated a musician who used to ask me to stand right next to him at shows and while out at clubs. He wanted me to be a trophy to show off. At first I thought it was sweet that he'd send me to get my hair and nails done before a show. Later, I saw that he wanted to get his trophy polished and waxed so it would shine bright and compliment his bragadociousness.

When things started to fall apart in our relationship, meaning I started to call out the things that made me feel like a piece of meat instead of a person, I went to a show with him and he introduced me to his "friend", Nicole. Nicole came dressed in shorts that barely covered her ass and fishnets. I saw his hand slide down the small of her back as he introduced her. I knew that, although we weren't officially over yet, he was onto the next.

Did I throw a drink in her face? His face? Did I scream and yell? Did I call her a slew of names?

Nope.

I giggled, politely excused myself, slid my evening bag off the table, and did my sexy bitch strut out the door, head held high.

He ran after me, but I said nothing as I got in my car, shut the door, and left him standing in the parking stall where my car had been. I went to another bar, joined some friends, and we toasted to his stupidity. I ignored call after call for the rest of the night. And week. Then the emails, flowers, and facebook messages.

It's not that I didn't want to pull a Jazmine Sullivan. But I am a lady, and the best thing I could do is not allow his stupidity to make me change who I am and become less of a woman.

47

And honestly, I can't dream up anything he could say to me that justifies his complete disrespect to me. Nothing is more offensive to me than insulting my intelligence, and after dissing me like that, saying "But Baby, I love you," is doing precisely that.

I already *know* I'm better. I already know I was great to him. I already know my love is the shhhhhhhhhh......so what is the point of answering the call? Allowing him to tell me what I already know is a waste of both our time. What I also know is he doesn't care enough to protect my heart. He doesn't love me enough to respect me. Those things make it abundantly clear that he has no place in my life.

Running into him a few months later, I was happy, doing well in general, and he, clearly, was not. His career is still slumped, he is no better off than he was when I met him...in fact, he even backslid. I had helped him get several things in line in his life, and all had fallen apart after.

I don't enjoy that he isn't faring well now. But I am proud that I walked out, head held high, never compromising myself.

Stop *fighting* battles you'll never win. Stop extending your energy to all that is negative and harmful to you. *You are above it.*

And instead of trying to prove just how dope you are to the person by yelling, screaming, crying, and punching, let them see that for themselves. And trust me. *They will.*

Art & Fuckery

I have such an adoration for art, I find myself drawn to those who create the things I love most. I'm enamored by artists in general, but something about musicians always seems to just draw me in.

It's not just musicians, it's writers, painters, hell, even chefs. Anyone who can create something out of nothing intrigues me. And before I know it, I'm absolutely smitten.

Usually, there's a 30 Day expiration date on this type of infatuation. I'm no longer as amazed by whatever it is they create, or I'm still amazed by their work, but as a person, I'm simply unimpressed.

Of those who still were somehow magical to me after the thirty days, one-hundred- percent had the Fuckery Factor.

The Fuckery Factor is what is known as the hobby of "collecting women".

I don't mean this in a "Silence of the Lambs" way, I mean this in the "I can juggle many lovers, so I will, and do"way.

Over time, there was passion, a deep connection based on art (their music, my writing, sometimes collaboration on their music), and most of all, an inexplicable connection with all three. However, in the end, despite the depth of the connection (and an actual committed relationship with two), all three ended with me sitting on my kitchen

49

floor, fifth of whiskey in hand, feeling like a number.

I know that it's not right to say *every* musician (or artist) is a incapable of commitment or will cheat on their lover, but I am saying I just am done trusting the masses.

As an artist, I know there is a need for constant approval. Every time you create something and send it out to the world, regardless of how proud you may be of it, you are constantly under judgment and analysis. You are constantly at risk of being rejected. With at least one of these musicians, this was the case. Art is a difficult career to be in, and a constant "cheerleader" in your corner always makes it easier.

Additionally, there's constant access to masses of women. Sometimes, it's some super fine bitches. Sometimes it's just a lot of women. Regardless, they're ever- present, and constantly throwing themselves at them.

Last week, I received a zip file in my email with several new tracks from an ex-love who once meant the world to me. Our break-up was a bad one, and we were unable to salvage a friendship because of his disrespect to me. By the time I figured everything out, I quickly lost the passion for him, and it was like a ghost of my love haunted my chest, but the real, connected love I felt was gone.

It has been several months since we last communicated, and the sting of the breakup was gone, so receiving the music, I honestly was glad to see him moving on with life and was ready to forward his music onto whatever places I could to help him out.

Of eight tracks, only two really stood out to me. Both were slower paced, the hook was a little more polished, and the bars were sharp. They seemed most genuine, and he had really grown as an artist.

Then yesterday I got the text message. Those two, and another, were about me.

It ruins the music for me. I don't know if it was a selfish attempt to "move" me to offer him another chance, or if he genuinely thought the music made up for how I felt when I realized I was just a number to him, but it literally made me nauseous. Anger immediately followed.

The artists I've found all seem to have this high and low and never a middle. They either need constant attention and reassurance, or feel they're on top of their game and want nothing. They either need you right next to them or need you to stay the hell away. They want one woman to stand by them or want a thousand women to surround them. And you never know which is the "want" of today.

The factor I see in this is the consistent focus on what *they* need, and never an evaluation of what is best for me. Friends in relationships with artists all understand this when I've spoken to them about it in the past.

Of the artists in my experience, I'm friends now with one, and the other two have come back at some point trying to rekindle the flame. Unfortunately, when you piss on my campfire, I no longer want to re-ignite it, and will choose another place to roast marshmallows.

When I went through the breakup with this one, a friend sent me this song, and it helped me get over the frustration and remind myself that he's the one in the wrong, and that his actions weren't what reflected my worth. My choice to demand respect is what reflects it.

To Matt, thank you for your support and love. To my Philly, thanks for always reminding me of what real love is, and for being so protective of my heart.

To the one who sent me the music, the one who made me stand right next to your insecure ass on that boat last summer, and the one who "can't believe" I don't see how much you've grown, I hope you have learned a lesson, and I hope the next one you love is treated with the respect you should've shown me when you had the chance. The song about missing something good, only to find gold-diggers and snakes was my favorite, and I hope it brings you attention. Sometimes what you have becomes what you had, and all you will end up left with is wisdom or hurt. I hope it's the first for you.

Merry-Go-Rounds

Love can be like a playground. It can be the most amazing, fun place to be.

The monkey bars are the part where to take a big risk and open up to someone and tell them how you feel. Getting to the other side of them is a great feeling in and of itself. The swings are that rush you feel when you are with them. The slide is the is the sex because let's face it, you can't be at the park without the slide. That shit's fun.

Then, there's the merry-go-round. That is the hard times. No one likes to be on it too long or you get dizzy and sick. It's part of the park, and we all have to go on it eventually, but it takes a good minute and a half before you're ready to get off the thing and go home or go back to the swings and slide.

In fact, if you got to a park with just a whole bunch of slides or swings, you might try it out. If there was a bunch of monkey bars, you might try the challenge out. But if you've got a park full of merry-go-rounds, you'd likely be like, "This is bullshit. I'm outta here."

The worst thing in love is that you just can't avoid the merry-go-round. Really it's just part of the park. And even worse is when you overdo it and end up nauseous and have to leave the playground.

Most of the time it takes me a day or two to be over the fight and, therefore, the man. I know there's thousands of playgrounds to choose from, so I really could go find a better one.

It's harder when you really liked the playground. You think back to it and just don't get why it had to be so bad.

How can it just be gone in a flash??

It's harder to believe someone could be so much of a part of your life and could be such a close person to you, then be gone. Maybe I have too big an ego, but I really don't get how someone else could get so much of me, then throw a cold shoulder my way.

For the first time ever, I have someone that knows me so well, has been such a part of my daily life that I have to actually change my thought patterns to exclude him, and he went Ice Prince on me.

I don't believe it. But it's the truth.

I was driving across the state last night, and this Pink song came on the radio, and although I've heard it many times, I've never understood it so personally.

You think back to all the promises and declarations made. The "I never"s and the "always", and then are back in the moment when it's the opposite of everything you said and nothing like they said.

There's plenty of things he said that I look back and think were either embellished, not how he really felt, or just misunderstood. Although I find it hard to believe I misunderstood expressions of love.

And on my end, I promised to always be a friend, but in a battle of him stepping back from all this love he expressed with no intention of doing anything about it, and my position that I can't love him and be with anyone else, I've come to a point where I've thrown up the Great Wall of Jen, and that is some iron clad shit no one gets through. It's the only way I can try to love another or just have fun and not think about what I wish could've been.

I could send a big long email full of a bunch of shit that a)he doesn't give a shit about b)makes me look like a dumb bitch for saying and c)isn't constructive anyway because it's just rambling without a purpose, but instead, I don't. I just closed the book, shelved it, and walked out of the library. It aches.

I don't want to believe it, but I have to. And that's not fuckery, but it's definitely "suckery".

O.P.B.

O.P.B. How can I explain it? Other peoples' b.s. I'm
done absorbing the negativity of others. I'm done
participating in kid shit, being in the middle of two
peoples' war, and I'm also done picking sides.

I will cut out anything negative and refuse to be dragged into anything.

I am a honeybee. I just want to make honey. I don't want to be
bothered, but so help me, if anyone comes up swatting or playing
with my hive, it's that ass.

I have better things to do. Like smell the roses and share honey with
loyal loved ones.

The End.

Insignificant Others

Well, folks, the time is upon us. Valentine's Day.

And with this day comes the basic call-outs by women of their list of demands, ranging from chocolates to roses to diamonds and the scramble of men to make sure their woman (or woman and jumpoffs/sidechicks) are silenced by satisfaction.

I hate to sound cynical, but I just find the whole thing a bit contrived. I like romantic gestures in more genuine forms. I like more simple, meaningful gestures that are inspired by something random (or nothing at all) rather than a commercially marketed "holiday".

But what annoys me more than anything is the vapid, sappy, ridiculous texts so many of us get in the days surrounding this "holiday". The texts from lost loves and failed relationships...the ones you got away from, trying desperately to launch blow darts at you hoping they'll be mistaken for Cupid's arrows.

This year, I plan to dodge these tiny little annoying darts with a phone number change. And, if by chance I get one of these texts, I just may send them all one of the pathetic pics of random strangers' penises so many men seem to think is a great textual icebreaker. That'll send a message, loud n clear.

In closure, if one of your others was that significant, they'd be on your mind all year and you wouldn't have to cower behind a holiday to find the gumption and courage to make the move. If you're guilty of this kind of fuckery, #KnockItOff. And if you're a recipient of this ridiculous shit, take a stand and put the Insignificant Others in their place this year.

So here, readers, is my gift to you. My Valentine"s Day *Poemme.*

"Twas the night before V-Day, And all
through my phone,

Were Exes and Never Was"s

Trying to bone."

PALATE CLEANSER

10 Things I Don't Miss About Being in a Relationship

1. Coming home to find that you're out of something you counted on
(beer, toilet paper, blackberry jelly, Fruity Pebbles)

2. Getting "Dutch Oven"ed

3. Sharing a home with someone who doesn't
squeeze the toothpaste tube evenly,
puts the tp on the roll backwards
(or just sets the new roll on the cardboard tube..grrrrrrr)

4. Finding out the persons bad habits

5. Arguments.

6. Jealousy

7. Defending yourself in the two aforementioned items.

8. Justifying things. Any things.

9. Going into the bathroom after someone

(even someone you really love)

has blown it up.

10. Having someone else instill/attempt to instill their beliefs,

mannerisms, or quirks upon me.

NINJA SHIT

101 Reasons To Dump Someone

Ask my friends. I can find a reason to dump/diss/stop talking to/pull a Heisman on/pull a straight up Houdini on anyone. So, in the interest of laughter and making you all shake your head, I present 101 Reasons to throw the deuces.

101. Stank breath.

100. Putting the toilet paper roll on backwards.

99. Doing a shitty job of a sorry attempt to rap along with any of my favorite artists whilst driving.

98. Having bad ass kids.

97. Not taking care of their kids.

96. Being off beat in public.

95. Overly feeling themselves.

94. Having too complex of an order at Starbucks.

93. Not having an appreciation for Funk music.

92. Having patchy facial hair and still growing a beard anyway. (For ladies, having a beard at all).

91. Being a MySpace rapper.

90. Wearing Cross-Colors, Karl Kani, or Starter jackets now.

89. Wearing cheap cologne/perfume.

90. Blowing up the shit out of my phone.

89. Asking "What are you wearing?"

88. Asking "What are you thinking?"

87. Asking "Do you miss me?"

86. Asking "What are you doing?" when they aren't deserving of a status update.

85. Saying "You owe me a _____" when it was never offered up.

84. Sending pics of their junk when not asked (men only. Dudes I'm sure don't mind the ladies doing this).

83. Talking about/asking about kids when they have not/may

not/will not ever meet them.

82. Being bragadocious.

81. Fishing for compliments.

80. Trying to instigate jealousy by braggin on how many people want them. No one cares, I promise.

79. Nasty feet.

78. Socks and sandals.

77. Being rude to waiters/waitresses/cocktailers/bartender s.

76. Trying to fight everyone all the time.

75. Dissing my family.

74. Dissing my friends.

73. Dissing their own people. (Why are they your people if you're talking shit?? Where is the loyalty!?!?!)

72. Feeling themselves more than anyone could ever feel you. (This is here twice for a REASON, egotistical asses).

71. Namedropping.

70. Namedropping people they don't really know (My personal favorite, I've caught people in this one talking about people I really know....hahahaaa!!!)

69. Talking about 69ing me when they don't fucking know me.

68. Weak game.

67. Putting a Dub on the outside of that big ass stack of ones. We see you.

66. Buying roses. I like orchids.

65. Calling/Texting/IMing repeatedly even though I don't respond.

64. Minimizing what I do for a living.

63. Acting controlling. (or trying to)

62. Disrespecting me on any level.

61. Too long of fingernails (men or women).

60. Putting me in danger.

59. Bragging on putting their hands on other women.

58. Assuming anything, from how much I like them to what I'm doing Friday night.

57. Treating me like a dumb bitch.

56. Assuming everyone's a groupie. Yes, there are lots out there, but not everyone is one.

55. Not valuing my mind.

54. Wearing clothes five times too big or small.

53. Making mouth noises when eating.

52. Exceptionally excessive public drunkenness.

51. Thinkin I'll give the time of day when their friend is my ex.

50. Not having a sense of humor at all.

49. Acting like everyone around is a complete idiot/elitism.

48. Over obsession with materialism.

47. Lack of compassion

46. Nasty habits in general. I don't feel the need to specify.

45. Being ingenuine.

44. Loud ass finger licking when eating. Napkins, motherfucker!!!!!!

43. Not washing hands when leaving the bathroom.

42. Having a lisp/major speech impediment (Hey, I'm being honest).

41. Hating on other peoples' success.

40. Unreasonable idiocy.

39. Arguing when they are uninformed/ignorant to the topic of discussion.

38. Always being broke but at the club/bar/restaurant/party

37. Moochers

36. People who are in the same place as they were 12 years ago in every sense.

35. Stupid haircuts.

34. Dirty fingernails.

33. Over-jockers. Show some class.

32. Jealous ass people.

31. Takers. This is in general.

30. Racists.

29. Liars.

28. Thieves.

27. Being mean to kids.

26. Never fucking smiling.

25. People who don't watch cartoons.

24. People who only watch cartoons.

23. Showing up uninvited.

22. Being too fucking needy.

21. Having no goals/intent on pursuing goals.

20. Being all talk all the time.

19. Not respecting the fact that hard working people are busy a lot.

18. Not respecting the my time with my kids.

17. Disrespecting my dad.

18. Mouthbreathers.

17. Loud, shitty singers (who are serious, not singing in fun/as a joke).

16. Sluts and whores. This includes men.

15. Being closed minded.

14. Only listening to one kind of music.

13. Saying they love me too soon.

12. Referring to themselves in third person.

11. Overspeaking for themselves.

10. Dishing out ultimatums and demands.

9. Telling me what to do.

8. Asking me for money. (Get your own!)

7. Handing me money. (I got my own!)

6. Telling me to change my outfit/getting mad because other dudes are looking.

5. Being a dick to my male friends because they're jealous.

4. Snooping in my phone/computer. I'd probably show them if they just fuckin asked.

3. Spying on me.

2. Saying something with an expectation of my response.

1. Ordering for me/speaking on my behalf when you don't even know me like that. (Once I had a guy tell the whole bar I was his girlfriend when I wasn't....ps, I was the bartender!! LEVEL 7 PISSED!!

I know there's more, like the dude I ignored after the first date because he drank from a straw weird or the dude who posted up on my porch all night on a chair when I was out and waited up for me (WTF!?) but my blog would be too long. One of these days I'll post the nicknames have for some dudes and how we came

up with them.

Independence Day

Have you ever gripped something so tightly you thought your hands might stay that way forever? Even as your palms sweat, the pressure on your knuckles becomes unignorable, and then....

you let go...

You feel the fatigue of the muscles and the small tickle in your knuckles as they adjust to the freedom. As hard as it is to let go, the release of the pressure feels better than the tension of grasping something so tightly.

Letting go of something you adored sometimes seems like the most impossible of tasks.

I'm here to assure you it is not the case. Difficult? Yes. Painful? Indeed. It is also, however, liberating.

Free yourself from the frustration, thoughts of what went wrong, where you should've stopped investing, and #forfuckssake stop thinking about how great it would've been to never have had it at all.

Separate yourself from a focus on the negative and work past the hurt.

I know this isn't easy, and I assure you, I'm sharing this advice with you just as I'm giving it to myself.

It may feel like you can't, but you *have to*. It may feel impossible, but the only things that are impossible in life are the things you refuse to conquer.

Am I The Allen Iverson of Dating?

I gotta get something off my chest because it's making me crazy. Crazy enough to post a new headline. And so fantastic, I can no longer keep it bottled up inside.

Allen Iverson is a fucking genius.

For those of you who don't recall the famous "practice" speech, it's at the bottom of this page. I suggest you stop right now, go to YouTube, play it, listen intently, then come back and read the rest of this.

I came to a revelation last Friday night about the practice speech and relationships. After frustrated texts from a few nameless fellows, a few MySpace messages, and comments I quickly deleted, I found myself laughing. Cause we weren't even talking about the game. We were talkin about practice.

I'm on the social networking sites for *friends*. Not dating, not serious relationships. That doesn't mean I wouldn't, down the line, by the nature of fate, meet someone and more will develop. But my intent is to meet cool people. Period.

To me, all the flirting with people and early dating is like "practice". And since I'm not in "the game", it's just practice. I know, I know. I know it's important, and I'm supposed to be all engaged in conversation, etc, but we're talkin about PRACTICE. I never tell someone I'm in the game when I'm not. I never give false hope of what's to come. I say from the JUMP that it's just light hearted and hangin out. It's PRACTICE.

But somehow, these fellas seem to think they have some kind of right to get annoyed if I have my own life. If I have very little time to offer, or am out with other fellas, they get all butt-hurt. They think I'm kidding or something. Or maybe they think they're Larry Brown and that I gotta jump at their whim. I know...it's funny to me, too. I mean, it's strange to me, too. But we talkin about practice.

Now, when it comes time to be in the game, and some of you've seen me play, and you know I give everything I got, but we talkin bout PRACTICE. Not the game....not when it actually matters. We talkin about PRACTICE.

So, when the coach said I missed practice, yeah I did. If I can't practice, I can't practice. Simple as that. Nothin makes me want to skip a practice more than when someone's trying to force something that isn't there. If you want us to be in the game, then just say so. That way, at least I'm warned.

So quit talkin bout practice, fellas. If you want a puppy dog that follows you around and stalks you, go find one. Til then, quit talkin about practice.

I'm done. And I feel much better

Controlled Burning

In wildfires, firefighters use a technique called back burning (also known as controlled burning). They light small fires in or around the path of a main fire to reduce the amount of flammable material once the fire reaches them.

A while back, I read a letter someone had written their ex, and it was like reading my own story. She has lost all trust in men and relationships and is trying to find her way back to the way she used to be.

I am a controlled burner when it comes to relationships and love. When relationships go to shit, they're like a giant wildfire. They kill everything in their path.

I metaphorically light shit on fire and burn it down all around me so that when the big wildfire comes at me and tries to consume me, there's nothing left to burn.

If you've ever been deeply hurt or let down in love, you know what I'm talking about.

Controlled burning and back burning need to be done with care. I'm still trying to learn the difference between controlled burning and singeing the shit out of everything around me, only to start a structure fire and end up having to rebuild.

It's one thing to protect yourself from an out of control fire headed directly toward you. Lighting everything around you on fire to isolate yourself is a whole different story.

I am a seasoned pro at the latter method, but have been working hard to be less impulsive, more introspective, and more conscious of the old "every action has an equal and opposite reaction" theory. I've stopped when I wanted to push or pull and shushed when I wanted to open my big mouth.

So far, all systems are go and the firefighters are playing cards and watching tv at the engine house. Or, as I like to imagine, are shirtless doing bench presses, curls, and pull ups on P-90X bars. Ok, ok...I'm off topic.

Controlled burning, to a degree, is completely normal if you've been hurt before. So if this is the situation you find yourself in, stop, take a moment, and assess your surroundings. Determine if there really is a threat, and if you do, indeed, find one, be organized and level-headed in your process.

It could be the difference between catastrophic loss and a solid, beneficial method of protection of your heart.

Unexcused Absences

We all have a little Womanizer or Maneater in us. Some of us are just more developed in our skill set.

A friend of mine texted me this last night:

> ''Men are from Mars, we are from Venus. We need Rosetta Stone to communicate with them.''

It cracked me up because when I get the calls in from my guy besties asking for advice, they share the same sentiment.

Here's the bottom line on communication and what we need to remember when dealing with the opposite sex. I'm gonna tell you the same shit my Dad sat me down and explained when I was a little girl and was figuring out the difference between friends, enemies, and acquaintances. *Actions speak louder than words.*

Really.

We are so subliminal, we look into what the words they said "really mean" and we are so quick to make up excuses for others. We decide what they "really are trying to say but won't say". This is how people end up pining for someone for six years and then drinking themselves into oblivion one day while the other person is walking down the aisle with someone else.

81

Stop making excuses. *Just stop it.* There is no excuse for them not *showing* you they want to be with you (if they really do). There is no excuse for it. There may be an explanation, but that is a completely different thing. Confused?

How's this? A friend was dating a guy who she thinks she loved. (I say thinks because when things went bad she did hardcore mean shit...not said mean things or pushed him away...she did *evil* shit. You don't do that when you really love someone). Anyway, she got pregnant; they slowly became more and more separated. By the time she had the baby, he was MIA and barely communicating with her.

I explained (not excused) the fact that his absence in her life in general (not in the child's life...that's a different discussion) was because he was not interested and not into her. He clearly did not want to be in her presence, period. She disagreed and said he was waiting for her to come begging to him for his time. My response was this: *Why in the fuck would you want to give your energy to someone who waits for you to do all the work?* I meant that. There is no excuse for ignoring someone, there is an explanation.

He was not missing her presence and energy enough to reach out and say so.

And to further the discussion, I explained to her that the more evil shit she did in the last few weeks, the less he can be blamed for not wanting her company. I certainly wouldn't want to be around someone who was disrespectful to me or talked down to me. And she continued to believe that he missed and wanted her, all the way up until she ran into him and his new girlfriend at a restaurant.

When someone wants you, they show you. If you show them you want them back, it's the most simple of equations.

You like each other, so it's 'game on'.

When someone shows ambivalence, and you've thrown up the 'open sign', you need to understand that there is an explanation, not an excuse for their lack of demonstration of interest, and stop focusing in their direction. Do not excuse it with thoughts that "she's been hurt" or "he's kind of a private and emotional person". When you really *want* someone, you *want them*, right? You don't say "I really like him/her, but I'm going to text so-and-so instead."

The only time I recommend you text person B is when your person A isn't showing you interest.

No one should need to be reminded that your company and presence is wonderful. They shouldn't have to read a memo to remember to miss you. I like my morning coffee. I don't wake up, get halfway through my day, and say "oh, shit, that's *right*! Coffee makes my day so much better!" I *feen* for that shit. Without it, my day sucks.

And let's just say, if I could send coffee a text message on days when I don't get it and say "I really missed you today. It wasn't the same

83

without your presence", trust and believe I would. In fact, if you're still making excuses for that person, ponder this: If they really are just poorly communicating their desire for you, they obviously are a shitty communicator and you'd have a relationship full of confusion. And they don't make a Rosetta Stone for love. Trust me. I googled it.

When someone wants you, they don't just want you. They need you. They want your time. Your energy. You are like a fix they need. And come hell, high water, or another man/woman, they still are focused on that dopeness that is you. No excuses or explanations necessary.

I close this explanatory rant with this: You deserve to be, and will be, missed by the right person. And if the person you have in your sights isn't staring right back, you don't have a shot. So stop making excuses and find another.

I'll touch on the people who show interest, then retract, then show it again in a future blog, but chances are, you either are patting yourself on the back right now for having done the right thing and re-focused your efforts in the past, or you have a number or two to delete from your phone right now. Or perhaps you have someone you need to text and express your appreciation to.

Now go be that dopeness. And when you find your dopeness, excuses and explanations will be the last thing on your mind. ;)
Note: Someone emailed me and asked why I picked Percy Sledge

for that post. It's really simple....

I listened really closely to the words of this song....and I didn't hear "When a maaaaannnnn loves a woman, he goes for like a week and doesn't calllll...........then he plays some mind games....and dates someone ellllse"

Get it? :)

Ninja Tip #357: Buh-Bye

I'd like to offer up a ninja tip.

I have many I'll never share, but for those ladies, gents, weirdos, and giant-ego- havin-ass people who think no one could ever *possibly* be over you, here's the way to 'delete' someone.

Now we all know the basics:

♥ Delete them from your phone.

♥ Delete them from all social networking (ALL OF IT! Don't front like you can be twitter homies...you'll see them be all lovey or call some other bitch/bastard the name they used to call you, and you're right back in Cupid's torture chamber).</li>

♥ Delete saved texts if you're a sappy bitch and save that sort of thing. (Hey, I don't judge, I've been there myself).

♥Delete the call history (in case you've got them in there, if they call back, the name will still pop up in some phone models. This is a no-no).

But, as I'm a professional ninja, I am here to help you take it to the next level.

Did you know you can call your phone company and ask them

to block specific numbers from texting? Yes. You can. I have. The shit works.

Did you know you can buy apps from some phones that will block specific numbers from calling? It will send them straight to voice mail or, if you're really on some bitter shit, will pick up and hang up on them (ouch!). For Blackberry, Call Blocker Professional is my personal pick. For iPhone, I've heard MCleaner works. For other phones, I recommend getting a Blackberry or iPhone. ♥ xoxo

Last, and my personal fave, is the email block. Now I have gmail, which makes it so incredibly easy to field emails in many, many ways.

If you want emails deleted before they're seen, this one is easy. If you want them put in a folder you can access when wanted/needed, but don't have to see on a daily basis, this is simple as well.

Here's how:

♥ Click the box and select one email from said individual.

♥ Select "More Actions".

♥Scroll down to "Filter messages like these". (yeah, that's

short for *'like these messages that make you want to light shit on fire'*)

♥ Now you see the illuminated golden box of
goodbye, aka, the filter settings. Here, you simply enter
their email in the 'from', then choose "Next Step" at the
bottom right.

♥ Here you have several options. My recommendations
for the ultimate Houdini is to select "Skip the Inbox" (so you, your
phone, and your email inbox never even see it), "Mark as Read" (so
it doesn't even highlight in your email or phone), "Apply The
Label" (and create a new label that says something like 'fuck off' or
'only
open this if you're a weak bitch', for examples), or, if you're *really* a
G, you can select "Delete It".
♥ Then choose "Create Filter".

♥ Next, repeat this process, and I
highly recommend choosing their name,
any nicknames between the two that aren't generic (example:
honey, baby, etc are exempt) and place them in the "Subject" and
"Has the words" (do these individually for best results) and create
these filters as well. This prevents anyone speaking their name
electronically, or them getting to you with that letter saying
"PookieBooBear, I miss you. Love, SugaryBooBear" or whatever
lame ass shit people say to try to get the ball that is secretly
covered in spikes rolling.

You, at this point, won't be interrupted by emails, texts, or calls, much less comments on your Facebook status or a twitter timeline full of their

face. Thereby, making it easier to quietly follow the road ahead without the distraction of the temptation of that moment of weakness in which you backpedal.

Now go forth, young grasshopper, I have helped you sharpen your sword. Godspeed.

Yeah, So??

I mentioned the Feral Cat. This isn't a title reserved for men; it's simply easier to find men who fall into this category. There are however, plenty of women out there in this category.

I am one of them.

It's not something I'm proud of, or that I brag about. In fact, it really actually sucks.

Feral Cats, for those who don't know, are wild cats that are not domesticated. They are wild, and in most cases, unable to adapt to domestic life, even in the best of environments. I suppose that I'm more of a Stray Cat if you really think about it, since I've previously been (very successfully) domesticated.

Like a Feral Cat, however, if real humans get too close, sometimes I freak out and go hide under shit. Or hiss when I don't mean to. It's my natural instinct after a bad experience in a past home.

Feral Cats also don't have time to do bullshit domestic cat games. They're out in the wild, so they're not manipulating their "master" for an extra cat treat or for cuddle time. Feral Cats are straight up. Anyone who's domesticated a wild animal knows when they're ready to eat, there's a clear sign and they appreciate the food. When they actually do come around and show you affection, you really have reached a point the vast majority of other people never will.

Feral Cats don't play coy. You're in or you're out, period.

I'm that way, and most of the time, it bites me in my wild kitty ass.

8 Tips for those Dealing With A "Feral Cat":

1. If you are in for just a wild ride, say so, they're really *really* good for those. If you're not, be prepared to exercise a lot of patience.

2. If you *are* in it to win it (or think you may want to be), draw lines. You shouldn't get all clawed up and shit trying to tame him/her. Your heart will be scratched now and then, but if you tell them they've hurt you and they care, they'll apologize. ER..um...cuddle you.

3. Don't chase them, but always let them know you're there. It may take a while, but eventually, they'll come to you without you calling for them.

4. If they do finally come to you on their own and display affection, give the affection back and create space for them.

5. Sometimes when a bond is created, it's easy for the cat to get

too comfortable with you and decide to split for a while. If
the cat comes back, you may find yourself at step one. Since you're
human, talk to them and let them know you're glad they're back.
Make them comfortable again, and they may stay permanently.

6. Don't let a feral cat do a bunch of back and forth shit over and
over. That's called "using you for food and shelter" and you don't
have a feral cat on your hands. You have an imposter called an
"Opportunistic Asshole". You'll know the difference because real
feral cats have souls. They're just protective of them.

7. its ok to establish rules and boundaries with a feral cat as long as
they're reciprocated.

8. If you, yourself, are a feral cat, be prepared for a long road
ahead. Know it's worth it if you're successful, but that blunt, open,
feral cat honesty is the only way you'll get there. Give and take and
have patience. Most of all, don't give up if you're really interested
in the other feral cat.

Above all else, know that you may find that you're just not a cat
person. If so, it's cool. of all things Feral Cats are good at
it's moving on. If you find this out, be straight up. The good news is
that Feral Cats very rarely become stalkers. :)

Happy Birthday to My Favorite Superhero

Every few months, the subject of my ridiculous clusterfuck of a love life becomes a topic of discussion with my Dad.

He understands my fear of trust and marriage/commitment, but also urges me to find someone to share my life with. He supports my extreme selectivity when it comes to men to a degree, but still pushes me to give more good men a chance, and--most of all--to not give my heart to the wrong one.

Fathers and dads are two different things--fathers are the business end of parenting, dads are the loving part. A father will tell you to find a man who is smart and will take care of you. A dad will say to find a man who will love the shit outta you.

My Dad is the balance of both. When it comes to the rest of any discussion surrounding relationships, my Dad is now sharing information that contrasts anything most fathers tell their daughters. The funny part is, he says different things for the same reason--to protect me from being hurt.

My Dad's recommendation, which I really find to make crystal clear sense, is this-- Live in sin as long as possible.

My Dad has instilled a belief in God in my heart, so don't get it twisted. I was raised to be strong in my faith.

But in love, he recommends not necessarily getting married, but to live together--or, better yet, to each have our own place and spend time back and forth between the properties. He also recommends each person have their own set of friends in addition to the mutual set most couples naturally have. These are not to be a secret or anything-- just relationships that are forged by one side and light and basic to the other.

Financial stability, independence, and should be somewhat proportionate from each side, and there should be an intrinsic connection and enjoyment of the relationship, but never a *dependence* on each other.

And if someone does something really fucked up in terms of loyalty or trust, they are fucking fired.

My Dad wants the best for me. I assure you, if he could, he'd stand next to me and fight off anything ugly, unpleasant, or just generally negative. And despite the fact that no one is ever has seemed to be good enough for him, my Dad also constantly says when he meets the one that cares for me even close to as much as he does, he'll know, and he'll acknowledge it. He'll also pour a drink and coach the poor guy when he doesn't know what to do with me.

I think one of the biggest reasons I'm as comfortable doing things on my own is because I've been raised to do so. I've been taught that relationships aren't a necessary part of existing. They're an extra you can enjoy once you're complete on your own.
Being in a relationship won't make you a better person. It won't

make you happy, rich, complete, whole...it won't guarantee security forever, and it definitely won't help you find yourself.

Being in a relationship *can*, however, be a beautiful thing with the right person. You can be inspired when you feel empty, you can have that person to tell you things will be ok when it seems they won't, and you can have that one person whose voice alone can make you smile on the worst of days.

The hardest part is finding that right person, and I know that taking my Dad's advice on what to look for makes it so much simpler than anything I've had my friends tell me.

And I also know that even in singlehood, if I were to face the darkest challenge, the most evil enemy, or the hardest of times, I always have someone who will fight for me or by my side to help me come out on top--my Dad. And that in itself makes me feel like I can withstand anything. And I'd do the same for him

Happy Birthday, Dad. You're a real-life superhero to me, and I'm thankful to be lucky enough to have a father and a dad like you.

Some Call Me The Gangster of Love

Look. It's happened to the best of us. We've given our heart to the wrong person. We've sunk everything into something that went bust. And in the end, we sat on the kitchen floor with a bottle in our hand, stunned at how we ended up investing so much only to end up empty-handed.

I never do anything half-assed. Therefore, when I'm in, I'm *all in*. Unfortunately, the greater the investment, the more impact you experience if you lose.

The good news? I'm a certified badass in the art of getting over someone. I can, and have been known to, help almost anyone press the reset button.

Here are my recommended ten steps of Hetox--Detoxing from "him". (Men, I haven't tried these steps for men and Shetox, so I can't speak on it yet). The steps take different amounts of time...I'm able to do this in 48 hours. Some friends have taken up to a month. Also, some of us need the friend to help us be a savage in these moments. I can be a G about this shit. But my drill sergeant tactics have never let them down. Whatever the case, do it in order.

1. Delete his numbers!

This is *not* optional. This is step number one, and it is an absolute requirement. It prevents moments of weakness in which you text/call/reach out to him. If you're trying to cut the heart strings, you need to be disconnected, at least temporarily. If you need to have a friend save the numbers for later, that's fine. But you must do this.

2. Get rid of the reminders!

The gifts, sweet notes/cards/letters/saved texts have to go. Again, if you have to tuck them away, fine. But they need to be out of sight and reach right now. If you want to get over the heart ache, the things that will make you miss him aren't going to do you any good right now.

3. Choose your music wisely.

I promise you, this is a help. Find the songs that remind you that you are better off. Don't play the songs that remind you of him, if applicable, and don't play songs that upset you. Find the songs that help you soldier up.

4. Get off the couch and put the ice cream down.

It is going to do you no good to gain an extra ten pounds from heartbreak. Go exercise. Go run. Hell, go buy a punching bag and fuck it up! Exercise is good for you and gives you endorphins. Endorphins help make you happy. Ice cream does not.

5. Get out of the house!

Look. You're sad. You're lonely. You're frustrated. And right now, you do not feel pretty, sexy, or like any kind of vixen. But I promise, you absolutely *must* take a night out. And you have no choice but to dress yourself like this is the most important night out of your life.

This is your debut--your relaunch party! Take the time to perfect your hair, nails, toes, makeup...because when you walk out the door, you need to feel the best you've felt in months. Tonight is not about finding a new man. It's about celebrating yourself.

6. Do not focus on finding another relationship!

I am absolutely *not* saying to not take numbers, date, talk to other men...I'm saying let the weight of relationships burden other people. You need a minute to breathe and remember that men also can be *fun*. Not just a source of stress and heartache.

7. Resist all interaction!

I say this again. Do not--I repeat DO NOT (sorry to yell, but it's important) talk or interact with him (or his people!!). Don't reach out to him, and if he is calling/texting/emailing you, DO NOT ANSWER THE SHIT!!

This also includes deletion from twitter/facebook/MySpace if he's a real bastard. If he's not, but there's still heartache, just ignore any interactions.

8. Drink! (with the appropriate supervision)

Seriously. Find the friend, guy or girl, that will watch your back, allow you to have the most fun you can without drunk dialing, texting, or doing anything you may regret (this may include hooking up with--or not hooking up with--someone-- side note...I don't condone hoishness. But for some of you, this works.). A good friend knows what's best for you and will make sure that is exactly what happens. But most of all, getting piss drunk will automatically release the pressure valve inside you.
You're going to burst at some point, spill your guts and your emotions, and in the morning, you'll wake up hungover in the haze of reality and, to be honest, see how dumb all the fuss really is.

9. Reality check yourself.

Now you've gone to the dark side…drunkenness and emotional outpour. You've let it all out--you may have cried, sobbed, smashed stuff, yelled, or, in some cases, hooked up with someone you didn't really like thaaaaat much (Hey...you know it's true).

It's time to reflect on all this, and realize that you've allowed this person who has taken you for granted to drive you to that ugly-ass place.

You're too good for that, aren't you? Yes, you are.

10. Start your engine!

Now is the time to make a decision. Is it worth freaking out over, or are you ready to just dust yourself off and move forward?

You have dissected the relationship and you've been to a really ugly place. It's possible you'll find your way back there someday. But not with the same person. This one is a closed chapter.

You should have gushed out all the girly, emotional, crazy chick shit and now are feeling a bit more pragmatic. Yes, it's going to still hurt. Yes, you will possibly miss him.

What's important to remember is you miss the good parts of therelationship, not *him*. He hurt you/dissed you/was so dumb he took you for granted.

Now, you need to let him go. Walk tall, and know you passed the hardest part. You're not an emotional volcano. You're now past that part and you can focus on the next part, which is most fun...finding the new man...and soon you'll be enjoying the honeymoon phase.

And you can stash this little thought in the back of your mind: if you're a good woman, and you're a heart of gold, he's the one who's missing out. Not you.

Fraidy Cats

Love sucks.

One-hundred percent of people who have been in love have been hurt by it. Yes, I'm pulling that statistic out of my ass, but I triple-dog-dare you to prove otherwise.

It's the nature of the beast, the thorn on the rose, the big pile of dog shit on the pretty green lawn.

On the flip-side, zero percent of people who have never been (or currently are not) in love report having the balls-to-the-walls amazing feeling love gives you.

We are a captialistic society. If there were an alternative to that feeling, someone would be bottling and selling it.

I find myself to be relatively fearless in most situations. I'm great at looking fear in the face and diving right in, as if it's some kind of staring contest and I refuse to lose.

When it comes to love, however, I come to a screeching halt.

Two phrases I randomly stumbled across stuck with me this week.

1. Nothing worth having comes easily.

2. To get something you never had, you have to do something you never did. (Thanks @Nikki206)!

It really got me thinking about the fear of failure and breaking up. I"m sure it was amazing the first time the Wright brothers got their plane off the ground. The exhilaration was probably worth every single failed attempt to get the thing off the ground and flying.

I say it must be the same way in love. I've got the plane to the runway before, only to have the shit crash. I've got the plane going and had it run out of fuel. I've even had a bomb threat and jumped out of the plane and went running.

In spite of it all, I still want to know what it feels like to fly.
I have faith that I will experience the flight eventually. I just need to remember how to be fearless, just as I am in so many other situations in life.

And quit being such a little bitch about it.

jenburger

PALATE CLEANSER

41 Mistakes When Trying to "Holla"

These are not only places from which someone tried to get my/a friend's number, "holla", get at me/a friend, or just plain try to take me/friends home, but some are the techniques themselves.

Either way, they are among the stories we giggle about...some even several years later.

1. Outside the Department of Corrections office

2. While sitting in the obstetrician's office awaiting a prenatal appointment.

3. At the unemployment office.

4. In criminal court (she was a witness in a case, he was up on rape and domestic violence charges.)

5. While test driving a car. (He was the salesman, I was test driving. #Awkward)

6. While your girlfriend is in the changing room.

7. While she's with her dad anywhere (ex. I was at Home Depot with my dad. That guy almost got a near-death experience).

8. After you've done a shitty performance on stage somewhere and she was in the audience.

9. At a funeral of a mutual friend

10. In an E.R. waiting room

11. At a party the same night she dumps your good friend.

12. While you're being detained by police.

13. While arresting her boyfriend. (Yes. This happened to me)

14. After she's stated that she's not interested.

15. After you've been in a fight and clearly, incredibly obviously, lost.

16. As she's cleaning your vomit up at the bar.

17. While her man is in the bathroom at the restaurant.

18. While she's disconnecting your power for non-payment.

19. After being caught picking your nose at a stoplight.

20. While wearing a drink that was just thrown on you by another woman you foolishly hit on.

21. While picking up your Valtrex prescription (She was

the pharmacy tech...REALLY?!?!)

22. By doing a "sick" BMX trick. On a stolen bike. When you're at least 30.

23. While drunk and at the liquor store before 11 am. (I was there assembling displays. He was not).

24. While shopping for panties. (It matters not whether they were for his girlfriend or just for him. Fail either way).

25. When your girlfriend goes to the bathroom.

26. Hitting on your waitress and offering her a trade of her number for any kind of drugs she wants (Yeah, that happened to me)

27. When her boyfriend is your boss.

28. At the needle exchange (she was volunteering, he was exchanging)

29. After running over her dog in traffic.

30. After giving her dad a rectal exam (he was the doctor, her dad was the patient. WHAT!?!)

31. Hitting on the bartender after she 86'd you from the bar last

week.

32. By rapping to her (and doing a horribly shitty job
of it)

33. By showing her all of your gang tattoos outside the
Am/Pm

34. By grabbing her arm and dragging her over to you. (This
happened to me at a casino. Scared the SHIT out of me!!)

35. After being booed off stage by a crowd

36. By telling her you like her, then when she says she's not
interested, saying "I'll pay" and doing the "dancing caterpillar"
eyebrows

37. After a big, loud, public fight with your woman, where you call
her all kinds of
horrible names.

38. While being evicted from your apartment.

39. While in line at Walgreen's buying
Athlete's Foot medicine.

40. While doing the walk of shame from someone else's
house/hotel room.

And my personal favorite...

41. While hiding in bushes from the cops after stabbing someone. (I STILL can't believe it happened. But it did. To me.)

THINGS TO REMEMBER IN LOVE

Let's Set The Record Straight

Ok, as much as I rip on silly mushy sappy lovey shit (barf) I will say I do have a genuine respect for real, deep, true love.

I figured I'd balance out my page with a few brief shouts out to people whose love is so damn adorable I can't even pretend to be nauseated. A written demonstration that I'm not a hater, I'm a cynic. But I still appreciate that which is deserving.

So, here's my list of cute couples that deserve props for doing it the *right* way. If there is such a thing.

1. My friends Maryam and Al

The most adorable lovebirds ever. They respect each other, aren't all jealousy and accusatory, and genuinely love each other. Two of the loveliest people, and it's truly inspiring. Today, she put this on twitter:

"One of the most romantic things he does, every Friday he e-mails me how he proposed to me. To this day, I cry tears of joy each time LOL (= "

How damn cute is that?!

Major cute points, and props to them for having a love like that.

2. My great-grandma Marcellina and her husband Franco. "Marci and Lefty".

Every night after dinner, even into their seventies, they would do the dishes. She'd wash, he'd dry. And then he'd snap the towel on her booty and she'd give him a side-eye.

He was almost deaf and could hardly walk when he passed away, and she stayed at his bedside until the last moment, holding his hand. He shouted "Marci, this is it, I'm going!"

And she leaned in and shouted so he could hear "Take the elevator, Lefty! You'll
never make it up those stairs!" They both laughed through the tears and he took his
last breath.

They kept humor in the darkest of times, and I can only hope to find a love that amazing someday.

3. Sophia Loren and Carlo Ponti

What can I say? I didn't know them personally (obviously) but this picture alone explains everything about their love for each other. It's adorable and I love it.

Carlo was quoted as saying the following about Sophia:

"'"I have done everything for love of
Sophia. I have always believed in her."

""I knew immediately she was someone remarkable. Something
played off her that gave her a kind of illumination."

They were together from 1965 until his death in 2007.

How could anyone speak poorly on that?

So before anyone doubts that I have a heart beating in my chest, I
assure you I do. And perhaps comparing the flighty affections of
others to these kind of loves is the reason I'm so hesitant to
surrender myself to the concept of love.

Lost In Translation

Texting. BBM. AIM. Email. Gmail, Yahoo....

We've slowly adapted to completely impersonal ways of communicating with the people we love. Texting once was a great way to keep in touch with someone and have a conversation without "interrupting" them. It's a continuous conversation in which you can reply at your convenience.

You also can take time to think through what you'll say, delete it, re-word it, or just wait to reply until you know what to say, unlike face-to-face or phone conversations.

The universal problem with this is the fact that a tone of voice, emphasis on a word, a facial expression...even a touch...are not a factor.

One man's "Goodbye" is another one's "I'm getting the fuck outta here".

Last night, someone pointed this out to me, as we resolved a complete misunderstanding that has been going on for weeks with one simple phone call.

He had asked me if I could call him the next day, and I replied "Yes. Goodnight." because I was in the middle of a live conversation with my Dad. I was trying to make the text short and sweet, and did not think about the person on the other end of the line until I had hit send.

It bothered me so much, I followed up with a text stating that I wasn't trying to be short with him, but that I was mid- conversation with my Dad and that I wanted to clarify.

We can add all the smiley faces and lol's we want, but it still doesn't replace an emphasis on a word. If we capitalize it, it becomes text yelling.

Example:

Let's try to say "I need you to understand." And let's just say this is someone who is hurt and is asking the person to stop and listen to them, and asking for them to reconnect..

I NEED you to understand.

This sounds like you're yelling "need" and is overly assertive. It could alienate the other person and make them defensive.

I need you to understand.

Simple and straightforward, but it doesn't convey the fact that the person on the other end of the line is hurt, and wants to reconnect.

I need you to UNDERSTAND.

Again, direct, but overly assertive. Also, emphasizing the word "understand" could be misconstrued as an accusation that the person is too dumb to "get it".

See what I mean?

When really, a phone call would let the emotion in the person's voice demonstrate their concern and desire to reconnect.

A Skype or video phone conversation would let you see the person's facial expressions...maybe puppy dog eyes or just a slightly furrowed brow. And this might be enough to make it clear that they want to fix it, not end it or push you away.

Now I assure you, I have sent some texts to people that can't possibly misunderstood. "Go fuck yourself" is a pretty universal statement. "Stop fucking texting me" is another that is pretty difficult to take wrong, even for a stalker.

With communication being such a major cornerstone in any relationship, I encourage you to take the time to pick up the phone when you're starting to disconnect, have texted back and forth too many times, or if it's a serious matter.

I plan to opt in on a video phone, because talking on the phone typically bores the living shit out of me, and I get distracted. Whichever the case in your situation, think about ways to keep impersonal things from being the driver for things that are very personal to you.

10 Kickass Things EVERY Woman Should Do For Her Man

I'm not the easiest person to lock down into a relationship, but when someone is able to capture my heart, I have no shame in saying I'm a relentlessly badass "other half".

So, ladies, I present to you 10 Kickass Things you MUST find time to do in your relationship. Some need to be done constantly. Others should just be done spontaneously. Whichever the case, do them well. And do them in a way that is unique to your relationship. But #ForFucksSake, do them. Trust me.

1. One day, when he has a really shitty day, pamper the living shit out of him when he gets home.

 Now women want a bubble bath and dinner cooked, etc. But I assure you, no heterosexual man will be mad to come home to find you in some sexy new lingerie or a naughty school girl costume. Take his mind off whatever it is that went wrong with the day and make him feel like he is a boss. Sometimes that little boost is just enough to re-energize him.

2. Be the girl in the relationship.

By this, I mean, you can be strong, independent, a partner, an equal, but dammit, let him be The Man. Let him be the King. You can still be the Queen. You can still run shit, and be the top notch, etc., but I assure you, don't outdo him and don't try to run him. Men want a strong woman, but they don't want to be made to feel "less than" or second. **Side Note: If your man isn't worthy of the top notch big boss role, it's

your own damn fault for dating someone

that's Junior Varsity, so don't bitch at me about it.

3. Text him one of "those" pics.

Yes, you know what I'm talking about. Now listen, I know we've discussed this before...the talk in the prior blog about not sending "those" pics to people...so I'll say this: Send a pic without your face and/or tattoos, etc. And, if it's a newer relationship and you don't know how to be subtle, send a sexy text message. Whatever the case, send him *something* to be excited to see you for. Something that reminds him that you're more than his girl. You are his partner, and you are one *bad bish* that he *wants*. Now.

4. Keep his secrets.

I mean this shit almost more than *any* of the others here. If he tells you some personal shit, don't tell anyone. Anyone!!! Don't tell your friend and say "I didn't tell you this, but...". NO!! That is Privileged Proprietary Personal business and he told you because he trusts you. Don't violate that privilege. Just don't.

5. Stand by your man.

Don't let anyone talk shit. Period. Set anyone and everyone straight if you catch even a

whiff of negativity. In fact, if you're really kickass, you'll venture into that territory about his friends and fam (who are deserving, of course). But loyalty, dammit. I can't stress this enough.

**Side note, again, if your man is deserving of some negativity or you don't have grounds to tell haters to shut up, then, I state it again, it's your own damn fault for linking with a JV Squad member.

6. Find his dream and/or fantasy, and make it happen for him.

This one isn't as hard as it seems. NO, I don't mean his ultimate career goal, I mean that one (or one) special thing he's always wanted (or that he doesn't know he wants) to happen. What do I mean? Do the legwork, and don't just get him concert tickets, get him a meet and greet with his favorite artist. Get him the autographed jersey of his favorite player. You see where I'm going with this? Go one step (or ten) beyond the expected. Show him he's deserving of your extra efforts. And, trust me, nothing is more moving than seeing his smile when he gets it.

7. If you act like a bitch, apologize, and mean that shit.

Women, we can say we are stable and we don't lash out without reason, but I won't say that because I'm not a liar and I don't sell wolf tickets to people. Sometimes, I'm grouchy. I'm pissy and I'm bitchy. It's no one's fault. It's work or stress or life or money...or nature. Whatever the case, I avoid putting my guy through those emotions with the prior warning, but if I act like a beezy, even a little, I apologize and am genuine about it. Pride to the side when it's warranted. If you are "above" this task, you're "below" the privilege of a relationship.

8. Be a freak.

Let it out. Launch the prissy, missionary-only, lady-like stuff out the window and then shut and lock it. Of course, this is to only be done behind closed doors in your own privacy, but let it out. Blow his mind and leave him speechless. This is your job. If you want to pretend women don't need to do these things for their men, go ahead. But don't come bitching at me when he finds someone else who wins him over while you were too good to let the walls down.

9. COMMUNICATE.

I say this in all caps because I know too many ladies who stifle or sugarcoat everything and then one day end up in a huge fight because he didn't "pick up on hints" or "just know it". Men like to just deal in reality. Short and sweet. Tell it like it is. Don't bullshit, sweep things under the rug, hide your true feelings, or say something is ok when it's not. You save a 15 minute conversation that becomes a four hour fight later, and the whole time, you've done nothing but damage your relationship. Just knock it off!!!

10. Be a Queen.

By this, I don't mean be a pampered bitch. I mean carry yourself in a dignified manner. Don't be classless, trashy, and do not be a sloppy bitch. We, again, had this conversation a few blogs back, but I say it again. Be someone he can be proud of. After all, he is your King, at least for now, if not long term...or forever, right?? And just as I've said before, if you can't see him in this role, cut his ass loose. You're helping no one.

I still say, respect is critical in every relationship. As is honesty, trust, and loyalty. But those are just the cornerstones to a healthy and thriving relationship. You still have to make it exciting, and you still have to give him reasons to remember why you're amazing. And why he should do the same for you?

Mirages

Wikipedia says:

> "A *mirage* is a naturally occurring optical phenomenon in which
> light rays are bent to produce a displaced image of distant objects
> or the sky."

They're often seen in adverse conditions...say, extreme heat. Driving
on an empty road during a heat wave or out in the desert, people
sometimes will observe something that isn't really there. Wikipedia
goes on to say:

> "What the image appears to represent,
> however, is determined by the interpretive faculties of the
> human mind."

The same is true in relationships. Sometimes, in the most
adverse of situations, droughts and long stays in the
desert, we'll experience "mirages". We'll see trouble up
ahead--our lover being unfaithful, or leaving us, an old
problem resurfacing, or a friendship ending.

What's important to remember in relationships is it is easy
for this to happen.

Think of the desert like a darker or more distant time in your relationship--a period of disconnection. It can easily disorient you, and the factors combine to create the conditions for mirages, and you may find yourself seeing things ahead that are individually interpreted.

It's important to work hard to stay clear- headed in these times in the relationship. Don't act on something that may turn out to be a mirage. Instead, talk with the other person. It's better to be open and honest than to assume you're right or that the mirage is real.

I recently blew it bigtime on this one. I, in an odd time of disconnect in an important friendship, thought a complex combination of changes in a short time revealed a complete collapse of the relationship on the horizon. In reaction, I braced myself for the relationship to end, and brought out the armor for battle.

Well, what an ass I am.

It was a miscommunication. When combined with my assumption that every time there's a desert, I'm about to be deserted, well, I'm sure you see how the mirage easily formed. And I ran with the shit.

When I share my opinions or advice on this site, it's not because I think I know everything. It's because I've had some great loves, some shitty experiences, and have given my heart to a few shit heads and a few genuine princes. And the end result is a lot of lessons learned and remembered.

If you find yourself stranded in the desert, separated from your friend, lover, or significant other, take the time to stop and reach out to them. It's better to work through it as a team than separately. It's not likely that two people will see the exact same mirage up ahead.

And you never know, you just might overcome those conditions and come out on the other side closer than you were when it all started.

Slipping Away

When you're in tune with someone--a friend, a lover, even an acquaintance--you sometimes can feel when something's just "off".

It's not very often I feel so in tune with someone that I can, without seeing them or speaking to them, know there's something up. It's something that happens only with those closest to me.

My Dad is a great example. Sometimes I have an urge to call him, only to find out he's having a rough day. I have a friend who I lose touch with completely, for months at a time, and just as she pops up in and weighs heavily on my mind, I will run into her in a store somewhere. This has happened at least four times I can think of. It's amazing.

My (almost) father-in-law and I had a connection like that. I could call him and tell him I felt like the casino was a lucky place for him that day, and he'd go--sure enough, he'd win. When he was terminally ill with cancer, his last month was spent in the hospital in Seattle. One day on the way to work, I had an overwhelming urge to call him and just tell him I loved him. Sitting in traffic, I opted not to, as it was 6:30 am and I didn't want to wake him, as he was so sick.

He passed away that day, and although he knew, I always am a little bothered that I didn't reach out and make that connection.

Some people are more sensitive than others. To a degree, they genuinely *feel* the other person's presence, thoughts, or emotions. I'm like this with those closest to me.

I stumbled across the song "Stay" by Shakespeare's Sister in my iTunes today while on random shuffle, and it spoke to me in terms of this subject. When someone you love is slipping away from you, reach out. Fight for them. Hold onto them and don't let them go.

Sometimes all they need to hear is "stay".

Apples vs. Oranges

I'm not one to let others make decisions for me. It's just not my style.

So it came as no surprise to my friends when I cancelled a date for Friday that followed a date last night.

See, I sat across the table from a perfectly great guy, in the perfectly great restaurant. He opened the door for me, pulled out my chair, and then let me order for him. It was the perfect balance between "take charge" and "50-50-ness", which I found intriguing.

My issue? He's a top-notch, independently successful, handsome man.

Before you throw your hands in the air in frustration, just hear me out.

I spoke with him at great length about life, love, business, and goals in life. And I heard a lot about what he has, what he's earned, what kind of women he's dated, and what he wants in life. All were great.

But I didn't *connect*. I didn't feel chemistry. What I felt was the same thing I've experienced with every other man who is very successful or is in the entertainment business: the one-up-ness.

It's the most fucked up dichotomy, but I love the men that constantly are trying to make the climb and grind their way to the top...their tenacity is captivating to me. Unfortunately, every time that quality I find so sexy has been the demise of the relationship.

The biggest turn on to me is the man who is tenacious about making it. The biggest turn off is the excessive showcasing of what he worked so hard and earned.

One of the loves that stole my heart right from my chest ended up smashing it with the Mr. One Up mentality. He worked so hard, and I respected him so much for it. As time went on and he gained more and more success, the ego came. And then the Kanye "I don't like it unless it's brand new" mentality. The bragadociousness. I knew the sidechicks were the next to develop, so I left before things got worse. He plowed his way through who knows how many women, and ended up back at my door asking for a do-over (which I politely declined).

I always get my heart jacked by these types...let's just call them apples. Because at the end, it's always some kind of a "How do you like them apples?" situation.

The others are the oranges of the world. The median guy. He isn't so accustomed to women throwing pussy his way that he doesn't know the whole package when he sees it. Most of these guys don't take a good woman for granted.

The worst part is, there is no apple- orange hybrid. You have one, and then the other.

I suppose I have to decide which I want and be willing to wait it out to find the right choice, or end up back at the right table at the right restaurant with a plate full of apples when what I really wanted was oranges.

Play The Love Game

For those of you in a relationship, I'd like to have a little sit-down with you.

Why in the *fuck* do you make things so hard??

I listen to friends every day talking about their guy or girl and all the dramatics involved. They've left the honeymoon stage and are now in this weird, fucked up land called "reality". They talk about things like dinner at their parents, not liking the salad dressing the other one bought, and my personal favorites laundry/dishes/bills/clothes/dry cleaners/leases/rent/walking the dog......

Now I know that life needs to be managed, but let me shed some light on something for you...

What is the first thing most people say they'd do if they won the lottery?

Quit their job.

So if you're making your love seem like a job...well, I'm sure you see where I'm going with this. Jobs suck, so if we had a chance to be free, we'd take that chance and never look back.

So why make your love seem like a job and not like it is the fortune you've won?

Why not focus on finding just one thing to do every day to make your lover smile? Send them a joke. A suggestive pic. Pack them a lunch and write something cute on the napkin. Ladies...stick a post-it with a lipstick kiss on his steering wheel so he sees it when he's leaving for work. Guys, if you hear her start to go business on you and start listing the things you need to do, pull her in and give her a big, giant, pin- her-against-a-wall kiss. Trust me, she'll shush.

It doesn't have to be a huge, expensive gesture. Just keep the fun in the relationship.

If you spent the day thinking about that stuff, you'd resolve the laundry/dry cleaning/walk the dog/do the dishes/check the mail issues with one quick discussion. And be right back to playing the love game. Which, if you ask me, is a helluva lot more fun anyway

Rosebearers vs. Bathers

If you don't know to which movie I'm referring, please do the following immediately:

Stop everything you're doing

Slap yourself for sleeping on a classic

Watch "Coming to America" immediately

For the rest of you, I'm sure you remember the two. And they had two very distinct jobs. The vast majority of women can be combined into two categories...Rose Bearer or Bather. Now I'm not talking about bitches, so let's not even bring that into this discussion.

Rose Bearers, by nature, put everything at their man's feet. They'll make sure the little things he doesn't think of, like where he's walking, are made as lovely and enjoyable as possible. These girls cook, clean, do the laundry, make sure his favorite drink is in the refrigerator, his favorite food is there for dinner, etc. These are the girls who got wifed down at 24.

Bathers just get down to business. They're there for a purely carnal purpose. Just bizness. Bathers aren't really too interested in what he deals with out in the world, they're satisfied with that one purpose. They're still there, but it's just less heart. And for some men, that's all they want, so it's a perfect match.

I've approached relationships as both. I've started as a Rose Bearer before, and I've been more on the Bather side of things before. I suppose you can call me a Rose Bearer who's been trained to be a Bather before.

I have to say, starting out as a Rose Bearer has never failed me, and the relationship has been real and lasted the tests of time. Those people are still in my life today. Starting as a Bather, it either fizzled out quickly, or the natural Rose Bearer in me came out, and I knew it was time to go.

Looking back on the catastrophes, fizzled out flames, friendships gone wrong, and everything in between, I suppose it's time to throw both titles to the side and realize that neither the Rose Bearer or the rather ever end up the Queen.

And that means step up the game and be more discerning about who to consider for the throne next to me.

In the questions I usually ask the men I'm interested in, when I ask "Rosebearers or Bathers", instead of the hilarious long list of answers I get (the most special love I've ever had said "A girl who works two jobs" (hahaha!), I'll give my attention to the man that answers "The Queen".

Liar, Liar, Pants on Fire

This was a huge insult as a kid. You called people out for being full of shit. You publicly mocked their ass on the playground, made a scene, and a lot of the time, alienated the shit out of people.

And lying is not a desirable trait. No one seeks out someone to date, or even a friend, who is a really good liar.

So why does society predicate so much of dating on lying, or at least a lack of honesty??

I've thought for months that maybe it's better for me (and a great way to prevent stalkers) to just be honest about how I feel.

"I'm sorry, I'm just not interested in you". Or, "I really, honestly like and appreciate you."

I figured these would be great things to say...refreshing, even! I mean, just tell it like it is and show your cards. I figured I'd prevent anyone from becoming a stalker because they got the wrong impression that I liked them. Or, on the flip side, someone who I pushed away for no real reason but my own hangups about relationships would know I truly like them.

So, I gave it a shot.

As you saw a few blogs ago, I finally just told someone I really just wasn't interested and that I wish them the best of luck, but don't want to talk anymore. I also have told one person how much I truly appreciate them in general and have been taking time at least once a day to say hi and reach out to them.

The text to tell someone I was not at all interested pretty much didn't go over well, although I didn't add fuel to the flame by engaging in a text war. I just shrugged it off.

The other seems to be fine, and my only problem is an occasional worry that I'm becoming too attached or too dumb for reaching out too much (even though it's pretty much only once a day). I also worry that he may think it's just game. I've had texts from guys before that are complete bullshit, although very sweet.

My question is, are we as a society prepared to be/capable of being really real?? Or are we so accustomed to bullshitting our way through things to selfishly make the road smoother?

I worry that we're so used to being lied to, that we don't know the difference anymore...or that we prefer the taste of the lies we've been fed by others.

I still maintain that little kids have it right. They love simply and without complication. They say what's on their minds. They don't understand hating other people for no reason, playing games with other people's emotions, and being mean in general. Fair is fair, and anything else is called out. And if there is a liar in the room, they will be mocked for having their pants on fire.

The more I try to find answers in the adult world, the more wisdom I find from my childhood. So with that, I'm slipping on my flame retardant pajama pants and turning out my lights.

Goodnight.

♪ Every Time I Turn Around ♪ ♪

Punky Brewster's mom abandoned her at the grocery store. Then
Henry adopted her. While shopping with Henry, they got separated
and she assumed she was getting ditched again, so she split. She was
home packing when Henry shows up. Then...

They sit down and talk, and Henry reminds her that her past
isn't an indicator of her future. The fact that someone previously
abandoned her does not mean that everyone who is gone for a few
moments is gone forever.

'm such an ass. I tried really hard to pull the ninja and let someone go
because I misunderstood them and thought he was trying to split (I'm
such a pro at the Houdini, I thought I saw it coming, and tried to shut
him out and split).

Then sitting in my living room, watching Punky Brewster, I saw that
sometimes when we have a bad experience, we copy and paste it onto
every other relationship.

Like assholes.

So thanks, Punky Brewster and Henry. I get it, I get it. (Insert cheesy ass
80's keyboard sounds here).

It's Not O.K.

Comfort is a two-way street in relationships.

Today I sat at a table full of "ladies" who are all married or in long-term relationships. I sat, shocked, in the corner of the table as I listened to them all discuss daily life and the things they're "glad" they don't have to do that I as a single woman have to...things like "keeping my legs shaved every day" and making sure I'm put together well every day.

Ummmmm, whatttt???

I couldn't help it...I had to check 'em. When did shaving your legs frequently become something to consider skipping (under normal circumstances, of course)? When did an Amazon jungle become an option in the land of lady parts? And when did we start trying outright "man shit" out in relationships??

I'm sorry, you can call me an anti-feminist because I think a woman should be just that--womanly--in life and in relationships. I will wear that badge on my smooth silky lotioned legs and raise my hand to claim it and show off my perfectly groomed underarms.

In fact I'm gonna go stand directly in the line of feminist fire and state that it is not an "option" to be as close a version as possible of the woman we were the day they met us ten years down the road.

"Comfortable" in a relationship should be wearing sweats and a wife-beater around the house but still have them fit properly, have your hair combed/groomed/tended to, and have your toes looking like pretty little lady feet instead of eagle talons.

You laugh, but I've seen friends who let it all go just because they found a man they love and feel they've done all they need to do.

I was once with a man for almost seven years. I took care of myself on day one, and on the last day, several years later, I looked damn good as I gave him one manicured little middle finger and some walking papers. I was never a sloppy bitch.

The ladies at the table assumed I was saying this not out of genuine belief that we should be taking care of ourselves and presenting an attractive package to our man, but out of fear that some other well-groomed chickie would show up on the scene and steal him away.

Let me state for the record, as I did for them, that this is wrong. To. The. Fullest.

Do not get me started about "keeping a man" or "ways to prevent them from cheating" because

I don't do this

I don't give a shit about the subject. Someone cheated on Halle Fucking Berry. Case closed. No one is exempt from the possibility.

If you're worried about that, you either already have a cheater or you're about to fuck up a relationship by letting this be a focus.

I discuss these matters because I feel if you love someone (or shit, even kinda care about them) you will do these things out of basic respect.

I drop my children to school every morning, and I make damn sure my hair is combed, my clothes are matching and presentable, and I am well-groomed. I refuse to disrespect them by presenting anything less than that.

I am not saying we all need to take hours to get ready, or that we all need makeup artists to help us be photo-shoot ready every day, but daaaaaaaaaamn, Giiinaaaaaaaa!!! Show some pride in yourself and give your man a reason to look at you and want to get you in a shower to do things with you, not just to make sure you are using soap.

Ladies, just remember the "Sloppy Seconds" rule:

If you're sloppy, take a few seconds and handle your scandal.

Sloppy Beezyness is not, nor will it ever be, o.k.

Thank you. That is all.

What You Doin?? Bullshittin.

Men and ladies do it, so this isn't an anti- man blog post.

Whatever happened to honesty? Why do people beat around the bush, not say what they really feel or really want??

I've been through it countless times, and I'm watching friends go through the same. Ladies play interest in a guy, then keep dating other people, or cheat on their boyfriends. Men are saying they love the lady, then diss them or take them for granted. Phones are blowing up with other people, sometimes people who don't know they're talking to someone who already has a relationship.

What happened to leaving? What happened to saying, before there's animosity and anger, before there's bitterness from betrayal, "I just don't want this anymore"???

I've never dragged on a relationship I didn't want to be in. I never made future plans with someone I didn't want to make plans with. And, most importantly, I never was so disloyal to feign interest in a man, just to diss him behind his back.

Honesty is the cornerstone of any relationship. Trust, faith, and happiness in general all teeter on honesty. When that is breached, everything else is a fast slide to disaster.

And don't drag things on with a pretense that "someday" it'll be ok, or "someday" you'll come back. Just go. Spit it out. Say the words. Unless you think you're sooooooooooo dope the other person should sit curbside and wait for you. Because I'm here to tell you, as a friend, no one should wait for anyone else to "figure out" how much they love someone. It's one of those things you *know*.

So Woman Up! Man Up!! Slide on the big boy/big girl pants, and speak your mind!!

You're grown, be about it!

I absolutely call out and challenge anyone reading this blog who is being dishonest to another to just make that call today. Call and say "I'm all in" or "I'm out" or even "I don't know what I want anymore, but I can't do this the way it's been being done anymore."

Quit the bullshittin.

Trust me, it may be tough to do, but when you're living freely and doing it straight up, it's like you have wings.

Soldiers

We're tougher than we're given credit for. Those of us who brave the roughest terrains in the name of love. We stand back up after being kicked, punched, stabbed, shot...we're never really truly defeated.

There are people out there to hurt you. There are people that enjoy exercising control, holding shit over your head, or doing things just so they can remind you of all they do.

There are people who choose us for a purpose in their life--to show us off, to have us boost their self esteem or egos...sometimes just to use for anything they can get.

It's hard, and it's easy to want to give up...to be done, to throw down your armor. It's also sometimes tempting to smash through the masses slicing everyone with your sword and gutting them all.

The strongest use love as their fuel. Love past the hurt, love past the pain, and let it carry us through it all.

We are the ones who get through it all. And when the battle is over and the masses have all sliced each other to shit with hate, anger, and motives, we'll be the champs.

So soldier up, lovers of the world. We're gonna be ok.

PALATE CLEANSER

Today Was A Good Day

People are always complaining about the misogynistic connotations of rap music. The out of control violence. The references to being an out of control citizen. Well, bitches, I've got news for you.

Pay attention to **I**ce Cube's ''Today Was A Good Day''.

I've listed, in order of appearance, the wholesome subjects Mr. Cube touches on. Buleeeeeedat.

1. Recycling.

He makes great use of an old Isley
Brothers beat.

2. Religion/Praising God

He wakes up, and the first thing he does is say hello and thanks to the man upstairs.

3. Healthy Eating Habits

First, momma cooked the breakfast with no hog. Then, he notes that he got his grub on, but he didn't pig out.

4. Goal Setting

He hooked it up with a hottie. He also hooks it up with Kim. Because that girl apparently can fuck allllllll night.

5. Appreciating Valued Possessions

He has pride of ownership when he makes the assssssssssssssss drop.

6. Valuing Friendships

Ice Cube doesn't

lose touch with friends and loved ones over time. No. He calls up the homies, and finds out whats really good.

7. Police

Well, I hear nothing about him wanting to kill any. Word. ♥Cops♥

8. Appreciation of the Arts

He watches a cultural arts showcase, Yo MTV Raps! At ShowDogg's house.

9. Mastering Skills

He owns everyone at some Craps, then follows that shit up
on Dominos.

10. Realizing Your Dreams

Regardless of his desires in High School, Cube comes through in
his twenties by fucking the girl he's been trying to hit since the 12th
grade. Never give up on your dreams, people.

11. JIMMY!!! :) (Hi, Jimmy)

12. Indulging in Moderation

He picks himself up a Fat Burger after a long, hard day.

13. Self Discipline

Cube may be drunk as hell, but he's certainly not throwing up.
It's all about knowing when to say when.

14. Self Discipline, part 2

At the end of the day, he didn't even have to use that AK.

jenburger

KID SHIT

Your Five-Year-Old Self Needs To Be
Your Co-Pilot

Every one of us has a five-year-old self. Some of us stifle them, some of us let the little bastard run our lives. But smart people let their five-year-old-self be their co-pilot when things get too complex.

What the hell do I mean?

Well, check it out. We as adults make everything more difficult than it needs to be. Some of us try to be so intelligent about every decision or action that we become fucking philosophers and add all these hypothetical endings and complications to some matters. Then we get caught in these debates.

Case in point, my friend who we'll call A. A recently had a baby with someone who is letting his five-year-old-self run every decision he makes. He's an ass and is off throwing tantrums and not participating while she sits back waiting for him. When his five-year-old-self feels cuddly, every few days, there he is at her door wanting to play house for a few days.

So, as A sat on my couch asking me to help with her decision "What do I do??" "But he used to be such a great guy" blah blah blahhhh, I encouraged her to let her five-year-old-self step in.

A kid would say "Why would you want to be friends with someone who's mean?" or "Why would you play with an Indian Giver? He's giving his heart then taking it back."

The age of five is the best age for this common sense with a grip on reality. Lots of people get all fucked up in childhood. But age five is when you still have some faith in the world (for most kids).

Anything before is unrealistic and you haven't had enough playground time. Anything after becomes too complicated. Five is when the opposite sex hits you it's because they're pissed, not because they "secretly like you". Five is when you enjoy everything with an open mind and an honest heart. Five is when you have faith that there are good things left in the world. And five is when you know when to put down your toys and go somewhere else when a "friend" is being an asshole.

A five year old will tell you the following:

If you hate doing that, you just shouldn't really do it. Unless you have to.

If they're mean to you, you should break up with them.

If you like them, you should just send them one of those "Yes or No" notes.

Don't be friends with people who boss you around.

Lying will get you into trouble. You should be a
good friend.

When you're mean to someone you should
say you're sorry.

If you're single, let it judge whether you give your heart to someone.
It's a bottom line. Do they like you and do you like
them back?

And if you're in a relationship and you're in a rough spot or a fight,
keep it freaking simple!! Don't be mean, say exactly what you feel, and
for fuck's sake, remember you both have a heart at stake!!!

I could go on, but my five-year-old-self says its Saturday and I
should go outside and play.

Air Your Dirty Laundry

What better way to lighten the deeply serious content of my last blog with a discussion about the analysis of human behavior and farts.

While it's true, I'm not the most ladylike of people in some instances (for example, my deep adoration of profanity), I do have couth, and I do have some things I find to be poor etiquette...like farting in public (intentionally), and hiding it from other people (within reason).

And while talking with someone a little while ago, we discussed this person "sneak farting" at the grocery store with me. I wanted so badly to call them out, but I didn't until they had gotten away with it for quite a while.

This person, who I adore, keeps their feelings really bottled up and tends to minimize/hide their mistakes, and often won't admit to anything when told they're wrong.

We instantly realized the correlation. We applied it to other people...

My oldest daughter and I and my friend are the same. We won't go out of our way to do it, will of course not publicly let it out without shame, but if we *do* slip, we'll excuse ourselves. In life, we will admit to our mistakes, but be real and recognize we're human beings and aren't perfect.

We continued.

My grandma insisted, to her death, that she did not fart. Had never farted, was incapable of farting, and anyone suggesting otherwise was horribly in the wrong. She also, in life in general, was someone who lived in *complete*, to the point of mental illness, denial.

My ex thought it was funny to fart, loudly, at the grocery store and, loudly announce "Baby!!! Nasty!!" at me, making others think I had been the one ripping ass in a public setting (never in my life, thank you!!). In the end of our relationship, despite the fact that I left him for a reason list longer than Santa's Naughty &Nice list, he blamed me to all our friends. And, just like when people looked at him knowing I hadn't farted in the cereal aisle, our friends knew better, too.

Just like in life, you have people who won't accept blame for anything, people who are constantly in breach of everyone else's peaceful enjoyment of life...people who live in denial, people who accept faults, people who have such low self- esteem they'll go out of their way to conceal things that are just natural to being human...

They're all there. And when they fart, whether or not they know it, they're figuratively "showing their ass".

The Art of Not Giving A Fuck

IDGAF.

It's the most liberating phrase that could ever spring from your lips, yet it's so inappropriately used, it's begun to lose its meaning...thus, losing its power.

In a random discussion with a friend last week, the use of this phrase came up. And we agreed that typically, the people announcing this phrase most often actually give the most of a fuck. Or whatever the opposite of "not giving" one is.

The people who announce this, and really try so hard to inform everyone they don't give a fuck, clearly give a fuck that everyone knows they don't give a fuck.

Still with me?

It's like the people who always talk about how real they are. Or the people who say "I swear to God" and keep saying "on everything" "I swear" "trust me". Look, one time will suffice. We'll get the point. Anything past that, and you're not advertising, you're spamming us.

Not giving a fuck is possible, and quite often, I'm kinda good at it.

Before you compare me to the above- referenced fakers of the funk, let's clarify:

I always give a fuck about the people I love

I always give a fuck about money. Mine in particular.

I give a fuck about how I look, but am not overly giving of the fuck--just conscious of being presentable.

I give a fuck about keeping dumb shit out of my life.

What I don't give a fuck about:

People with agendas, particularly when they want me to play a role in them.

Dumb bitches and their gossip/skeevy shit/hateristic ways/general hoishness.

Men that just want ass (there's so many women willing to spread their legs for you, why waste effort trying to get me to?)

The shitty mixtapes crammed down my throat on twitter
(I like the good ones though)

How little of a fuck others give.

There's more, but we don't have time to go into all the things I
don't give a fuck about. We do, however, have time to discuss the
ancient art of Not Giving A Fuck.

Not giving a fuck means you stop any and all interest, feigning of
interest, or discussion of interest immediately. Typically stating "I
don't give a fuck" is a great way to do this. It should immediately,
without exception be followed with the actual act of not giving
a fuck.

By this I mean, no further discussion or consideration of the topic.
None whatsoever, and if the person you're with continues to bring up
the topic, not giving a fuck is far past not giving a damn (or shit, etc)
and you must qualify your level of apathy immediately by making a
clear statement such as:

"Did you just hear me?" "We're done discussing
this."

"Shut the fuck up already."

or (my personal favorite)

"I don't have a fuck to give about it/him/her, so stop trying. There's no foreplay for apathy."

The ability to cease all emotional response isn't key here...it's not having it in the first place (in regards to whatever the thing/person you don't give a fuck about). Guilt is non-existent, consideration is non-existent.

If you have any of the above listed items, or are still thinking on the matter, you clearly give at least somewhat of a fuck.

So let's just stop all the nonsense and start saying "I'm really trying to not give a fuck right now", or "I don't want to talk about it anymore".

But no more saying "I don't give a fuck" unless you, indeed, do not.

And now, back to our scheduled programming.

LOVE. LOSS. LIQUOR.

Fighting My Inner Ninja

I am a woman of stealth and speed. I can slip out in the night and disappear from a man's life with unparalleled skill.

I am just got done fighting that urge. The urge to slip away. To pull my chips off the table and GTFO.

The irony is, a good friend of mine, who is a lot like me-- independently raising her son, very career minded, and not a fan of commitment and giving into relationships--was going through the same struggle just a few days ago.

We talked, and the same concerns, fears, and doubts that had been multiplying and taking over my brain came slipping through her fingers into text messages.

A great guy, who she felt was honest and up front, who had his own concerns about her slipping away from him, and who overall she really, *really* liked and felt strongly for was in her life and all she could think of was what could go wrong, or how she might not have enough energy to dedicate to the success of the relationship with all her need to focus on keeping work going strong.

And, as I read all she had to say about him, and thought about all I'd heard before, I really wanted her to stop all this doubt nonsense and go in just as strong as she had gone in with her career. I felt like she deserved that happiness, and to be with someone who really makes her happy (and isn't a complete ass).

I gave her my opinion....that she should not push him away because of what "might" happen, but open up to him. He seems like a great guy, and while no one is perfect, come on....he's amazing!! If she's smiling just talking about him, she really needs to go all in.

Then I thought about the advice I was dishing out.

And the person who makes me smile like that. Who inspires me to work hard because he does too, and who doesn't get threatened or pissy about me working, but encourages me to go get it!!

So I decided to pull a real ninja move.

I'm staying in to fight the doubts. A real ninja doesn't sneak away from a potential battle. A real ninja doesn't pull a bitch move and slip away, or think "What if that other guy busts out a machete and slices my heart?"

A real ninja goes in, knowing the stakes, and comes out on top.

So, I'm slipping on my ninja mask and am sneaking up behind my inner ninja and taking her out. I'm on some countermeasures to take her sabotaging ass out.

I shared this decision with my friend, who oddly enough, was inspired by my decision to stop letting my inner ninja divert me from happiness with ninja star shaped doubts or blasts of metsubishi (blinding powder).

But more importantly, I was inspired by my renewed strength and fearlessness of what may be on the horizon for me. An uncompromising faith that all will be the way it's supposed to be no matter what.

And that, my friends, is some real Shaolin Shit.

The Strongman Competition

Have you ever watched a strongman competition and stared in amazement as a man...a human being...pulls an airplane with a rope and his bare hands?

Watching a man put up with my shit is like watching that.

When I say "shit", I don't mean cheating, evil shit, breaking of stuff, etc. I mean my strongwoman display of emotionally shoving them to the door with everything I have inside. When I'm hurt or vulnerable, I'm fantastic at scratching and clawing the living shit out of everything around me to create space for myself. And usually that means hurting others. In fact, as completely ignorant and fucked up as it sounds, the more I care, the more I want them out.

The funny thing is, if someone gets far enough in and get close enough to hug me, they win. It's rare that they can withstand all the clawing and fighting and still be standing there when I run out of energy to fight or give in. I don't want them to leave, but I don't trust that they'll stay. So when I get pissed that I care and think they aren't capable of the strongman competition, I try to kick them out. I know it's not right, but it's honest. I've allowed the uglies of the past to cast a shadow on some of the pretties I stumble across.

Usually, I'll find a song and stick it at the bottom of the blog just because.

This time, I have deliberately chosen a song that brings that shit to life. The words are perfect, and I couldn't identify with them more.

Even though the video is funny, it's still speaking the truth. Slicing and cutting and wounding someone who's strong enough to endure it and still stand is only going to make that strongman find his way to the door.

If you have a strongman (or strongwoman) that's stood through some ugliness that you've thrown their way, and they still are standing there, scars and all, put them on a pedestal and stop putting them through the competition. Just give them a medal and give them what a champion deserves-- respect.

And if you are a strongman, and you do withstand the early battles, you'll experience a heart that's stronger than the will to kick your ass out.

Meow. Purr. Hiss. Oh, Fuck It. I Give Up.

Ok, so let's catch up.

Since we last met, I've met someone, met and loved someone, fought off the return of LaundryMatt, drank Hennessy, acted like a top-notch asshole, hurt said someone, apologized, and then rinsed and repeated.

I could give you all the juicy details of the relationship, but I'm not gonna.

True to my style, I'll tell you what's most important.

He was super fucking hot. I mean tell your grandma to her face you have to go do some nasty things with a very hot man, wear your sexiest heels even to 7-11 just in case you see his ass, cast aside all previous standards you ever had for yourself hot.

He was a big, tough, caramel macchiato skinned bad boy. His personality fit right in line with mine...sarcastic, hilarious, all about business and making money, wild the fuck out sometimes and work your ass off others.

And we were practically inseparable from the start.

Blah blah blah, here's the rest. I cooked, we watched movies, got drunk, went out, ate out, did stuff, hung out with his friends, went to barbecues in the summer, laughed until 6 in the morning, texted dumb shit to each other all day.

When things got to the point where we were living each day in sync with one another..."Good morning. Want some coffee?" , text updates all day, meeting up in the afternoon out of habit, just crashing at the end of the night and doing it all again, things began to fall apart.

Now, I'm not blaming either of us. His inner dickhead met my inner bitch, and the result was "Jenga!".

So let's skip the dumb shit, and get to the fun stuff.

Here's how I got him back after he acted dumb, I acted dumber, told him to fuck off, then listened to what I thought were pretty genuinely sincere apologies, and a confession about really loving me and not being ok with letting me go. (Please don't puke, I swear it gets fun...just setting you up to understand my reasons to go to this extreme).

So, we hadn't spoken in four days. I lived in City A, and he was now living in City B, 26 miles away. He was in Scuba Diving school (yeah, really) and I was still bartending.

I woke up to another string of text messages void of his name. I lay emotionally defeated and buried under a big white goose down comforter, and slowly peeked my head to the surface, glancing up at the shelf with his things neatly stacked and his spare car and house keys laying on my desk. Damn, he hadn't even snuck in and taken his shit while I slept. Ohhhh, that's right, yesterday he left my spare house key at the bar under my tip jar while I was in the ladies' bathroom staring in the mirror telling myself to just fucking call already and say I missed him. I had missed seeing him by two minutes when he texted me to say he had stopped in. FML.

I had the day off, and lay thinking about what to do; get out of the house for the first time in two days...watch shitty daytime tv...eat a pack of Pop Rocks and chug a soda and pray for death so I wouldn't miss him anymore.

As I alternated between sighs and screams into my pillow, I stared at all the shit in my room that reminded me of him. And then I saw it...my power source...The Catwoman Mask.

In an instant, I had a plan. Somewhere over the next hour, I had gone from invertebrate failure wallowing in lost affection to a crimson lipped vixen in knee-high black leather stiletto boots, second-skin-tight black pants, a black button up blouse with an unbuttoned ratio of 2:1, and a cat mask bombing north on I-5.

It's like every plan ever plotted by Catwoman, the girls from Charlie's Angels, all the strippers in Las Vegas, and female Navy SEALs had somehow magically come to fruition in my perfectly groomed head.

"Hello, _____Diving School, this is

Lisa, how may I help you?"

"Hello," I purred. How did my voice become so incredibly sultry? "My brother is in classes today and I'm meeting him after. I don't want to call his cell and interrupt him during class...what time is the day over for students today?". I was fucking flawless.

"Oh," she chuckled. She had no clue who was tapping her claws on the other end of the line, "2:45."

I thanked her and hung up, just as I passed Boeing Field. I glanced at the sunny sky and cranked up "Return of da Baby Killa" by Brotha Lynch Hung. I had snapped and I knew it.

Cars passed, most didn't look over, but the ones who did took a fast second glance. I blew kisses to some and nodded at others. I had nothing to lose, including my mind.

Twelve minutes, six "Daaammmmmn baby!" shoutouts, and fourteen right turns (not necessarily fourteen, I just thought it sounded cool) later, I was in the school's parking lot. Twelve stalls, no Cadillac.

Shit!

I hadn't come this far to lose, so I pulled into the adjacent grocery store parking lot to reassess the situation. As I rounded the corner, there it was...the car I had helped him pick out just three weeks ago. I dug in the BCBG shopping bag in the passenger seat past his shirt (that still smelled like him....mmmm....ok, ok, distraction), his cds, toothbrush, the shirt he had given me to sleep in (which I had cut the shit out of and sewn to custom fit me...open backed and bad as hell), and the bottle of Hennessy VSOP we had bought over the weekend to his car keys.

One click and the lights flashed. I was in. I parked one row over because I'm no dumb bitch. I pulled out the cd with the perfect song that was silly and funny and poured out my apology for being so obnoxious and pleaded for him to not leave me. Without being too pathetic. (Thanks, Pink).

I walked across the lot with my sexiest strut, and with a proprietary flair opened the door and dropped his bag in the passenger seat. I glanced at my watch. 2:00. I had forty-five minutes to wait. Sigh.

I popped the cd in the cd player, skipped to the appropriate number, and turned the car back off.

Where should I sit. Passenger seat? Back seat? Trunk?

He wasn't answering my calls two days ago. It didn't mean he wouldn't today, but I don't call motherfuckers like that. I usually don't care. I wasn't about to be fired, and "time out" just never was my thing.

I settled on the back seat, and, seated sideways, kicked my feet up in the back window. But as I sat, it didn't take long to get bored. I glanced at my watch. 2:12. Well, this sucks.

As I sighed with frustration and dropped my head back on the back seat side window, I remembered I was in a grocery store parking lot. I decided to go get survival rations of some kind. Anything to pass some time.

I took the mask off this time, assuming I would be mistaken for an armed robber. As hot as SWAT team men can be, I'm here for someone else and intended on going home with him today.

I strolled through aisles, still strutting along, free from even the slightest concern about the judgment of others.

I settled on a shitty gossip magazine--the kind I don't read for a reason. As I approached the cashier, my glance was stolen away by the one missing link to my day of emotional lows, followed by insanity and inhibition...booze.

I snatched up the bottle of cheap white wine and snagged a bottle opener.

I swear the cashier heard the harps, too, because she smiled. I explained that I didn't need a bag and winked. She smiled bigger, as if she got the memo that I was balls-to-the-walls fucking awesome right now, in a mildly frightening way.

As I pranced to the car, magazine and purse under one arm, I cranked the wine key into the bottle's cork. Who needs a glass? I'm on a fucking mission here, and don't do "middle men".

I made myself comfortable in the back seat, sipping straight out of the bottle and flicking through the pages of smutty gossip I didn't care to engage too deeply in.

I checked my twitter, sent a few tweets, including one to a fellow badass, saying "In a Cadillac in a Catwoman mask drinking straight out the bottle".

And again with the magazine.

Halfway through the bottle, I noticed a small trickle of mid twenties hotboys coming from the other side of the lot. I glanced at my phone...2:47. Fuck yeah, it was GO TIME.

I continued flipping through the magazine, sipping away. I wasn't even nervous. Maybe it was the booze, maybe just my mental state, but I had to do it big or he may never have spoken to me again. I'd rather have him tell me to die in a fire than just disappear. At least then
I'd know where he stood.

In the swirl of thoughts and wine chugs and pages of "Stars with Cellulite" and "Lindsay's Binging" headlines, it happened...

The trunk opened.

Now I had butterflies. They were quickly chased away by an uncontrollable chuckle and fast inhale.....I think I had actually *become* Catwoman.

As the driver's side door opened, I flicked another page of my magazine and without thinking, the silky sultry voice I'd suddenly developed spilled out, "Meow."

He stumbled back from the car door.

"What the--"

"Yes," I continued. "This is happening right now."

He broke into laughter, put both palms at his temples and shook his head.

"You're unbelievable," he said, without a hint of anger. He was actually impressed.

Without glancing away from my magazine, I flicked to the next page. "I've been thinking. This 'time out' thing of yours is bullshit. It's just not for me."

He laughed and sat down in the driver's seat. He stared straight ahead, then turned again to look at me, as if looking away and looking back would have him find me with less cleavage and no mask.

He was still in shock, but very amused. I leaned forward, placing my elbows on the tops of the front seats.

"So, I've had some time and I've had some wine. I brought a song and your stuff's in this bag. After this, it's on you, but I just can't let you disappear like that."

He looked at me and his shock turned to a genuine search in my eyes for sanity, followed by the look I was used to seeing in his eyes--the one I loved.

His gaze dropped down to the nearly empty bottle in my hand. He snatched it up.

"You drank this whole bottle?!"

Hiccup. "Yep."

He shook his head and turned on the radio. Line by line, he chuckled through the first chorus and turned around, looking at me again with simultaneous shock and adoration.

"I told you that you were stuck with me forever," he said.

I sighed. "Fuuuuuck."

He laughed.

We were ok, finally.

==========

Another month followed, but his fear of intimacy and my strategic and involuntary destructive side slowly became greater forces than our love for each other, and within two months, we were no longer in each others' lives.

He was the male version of me. I had met my match, in the realest sense of the words.

As sad as it is to say he's gone, it's for the better. I won't bullshit you and say I don't think of him, and every once in a while I have a dream where I smell his skin as if I'm right there on a hot summer night curled up at his side. But when I wake up, I quickly overcome the love hangover, and go on with my day.

He's the chapter I missed in this blog. The delicious dish I should have shared with you, but didn't until it was all gone with leftovers condensating in a chintzy to-go box in the back of the bottom shelf of the fridge.

I suppose that's how it's supposed to be, because had I stopped to blog, we all would've known it couldn't have been that great if I was willing to share it.

When It Rains

I've been in a sunny, warm, beautiful climate for the last
month and a half.

With the ups and downs of love, every day I wake up to sunshine,
birds chirping, and if there's a cloud, it's a tiny fluffy white one dancing
in the sky...the kind that make you believe clouds are like cotton candy.

Yesterday, after a week of being the most savage, wall building ninja, I
successfully put myself in a mindset to lock out anyone who posed a
threat (aka, made me feel anything negative) and, in the process, tossed
a wall up at everyone else.

After days of silence between someone and myself, following my
email saying I just want to be away and not deal with him because of
heartache, I got a reply to the email as I was walking to my truck at
the grocery store. I scrolled my phone, reading the email.

It was a reluctant acceptance of my request.

After so many days, and knowing I had been hurtful in pushing
him away, I decided to call on the drive home and at least have the
respect to discuss it via phone and apologize for my harshness--
even ask how to smooth it out a bit.

I was met with the same coldness I had given.

As the harsh apathetic words spilled from his mouth, big, giant splats of raindrops began splashing on my windshield. I mean, large enough that I sat at a stoplight looking up through my windshield at the sky. Was God holding a giant fire hose???

As the call ended, and I accepted the state of the union, I stepped out of my truck and stood in the driveway letting the giant pouring of rain pound on my head.

The thunder started in, and I stood there feeling like I was getting the message from The Man Upstairs. I create my own thunderstorms. I can take the most beautiful weather and isolate myself and push everyone out, but all I'm doing is choosing a rainy day for myself.

The rain continued for over two hours, with thunder and lightning crashing around me, and I sat in the house frustrated, hurt, and angry. The outside weather was so reflective of my mood, it felt like a movie.

I need to remember that sometimes it's just gonna rain, and there's nothing you can do about it. You can, however, keep the people you love close to you and not push them away. That way, when it rains, you can stay inside and enjoy the indoors for a while instead of staring out the window feeling trapped.

Rain is there to clean things. It splashes the dirt off leaves and flowers, it streams dirt and leaves down the gutters to the downspouts, and it waters the trees and other plants. And, in life, rain is there to hose down the crap and leave you with a fresh perspective on things.

And for that, we should be thankful.

I'm Trippin

Right after high school, I bought my then best friend and I a pair of tickets to see New Edition's reunion at an amphitheater on the opposite side of the state. I planned a huge road trip, camping...the whole thing. We counted down the days, so excited to see the group we grew up crushing on, and the long summertime road trip that would take us there.

The day of the trip, we got up early, threw on bikinis and shorts, and piled into one of my dad's kickass collector cars. We drove for hours, flirting with guys on the freeway, stopping at random gas stations, and singing to the radio.

When we finally got to the amphitheater four hours later, we pulled up to big gates that were locked. Not a soul in sight. I called the number on the back of the tickets. The tour had been canceled.

Insert sad trumpet sound here. Sometimes, you head down a road, full speed ahead, not checking your mirrors, because you think you're staring at a clearly drawn map.

You might pass a few signs and ignore them along the way. You might be seeing your destination on the map, and figure you'll continue forward to reach your destination

Sometimes, you're right, and you take the trip to arrive at your destination successfully. Lucky you.

And sometimes, you pass all the stops, and keep moving forward, only to see somewhere along the road, that you were wrong all along.

Love might do this to you. You think you're headed in one direction, on all the right roads. But somewhere along the way, you realize you're going in the wrong direction.

Sometimes you're foolishly heading straight towards something.

It might be a bridge that once existed, but by the time you're there, will be gone. It might be a destination that won't be there when you're arrive...a closed down theme park or torn-down hotel.

And sometimes, you're just holding the map upside down and you should be headed away from it instead of right for it.

I don't know if I missed a turn or ignored a "Road Closed Ahead" sign, or what, but I think I just pulled one of these.

So, I'm parked roadside for now, and I'm on the phone with Roadside Assistance. I'm sure, when I step outside and look at it from a neutral perspective, not from the voice in my head that says how I actually *want* it to be, that it was my fault.

I planned a trip to nowhere, stumbled across a brochure for an amusement park, and headed out, full speed ahead. And just the other day, found out I'm totally headed for a big, empty parking lot.

So I'll hang out for a few.

Of course, the phone rings, the texts come in, and none of them are a new vacation destination that are too enticing to me. So I'll sit roadside, enjoy the sunshine, read a magazine, drink some of the beers out of the cooler, and wait to figure out what's next.

But I recommend that if you find yourself here, don't toss the map and continue forward. Stop when you see all the signs you're heading nowhere, pull over, and reassess the map. Call a travel agent. Don't waste all your time and energy making your way to a trip you'll think of as a big letdown one day. You never know. Sometimes, when you stop, you end up meeting a cute tow truck driver or dancing the night away at a bar you never would've stopped at.

It Could All Be So Simple

Why would anyone let someone else make them feel like complete and utter shit?

I got a text from my friend "A" the other day, and she had lost her mind because her man has a new girlfriend and had called "A" a long string of shitty names. And, rather than recognize that he is a small man with big problems, she allowed his mouth to destroy her.

Why would she not cut the loss? He's the one who will truly be missing out.

And I don't mean that in the cliché way that so many girls spout out when a man dumps their friend. I really mean that shit.

In a world filled with gold-diggers, side chicks blackmailing men out of millions, skeevy bitches scouring the world for other peoples' men, the genuine woman has become even more difficult to find.

It's the nature of the world that when a man finds success, the bitches flock. The men in power positions, CEOs, ballers, etc become a magnet, drawing the attention of crowds of women. And with all the success, wealth, fame, and attention, it's natural for them to feel they have earned the right to have a gallery of women...the wifey, the sidechicks, the quickies...it's all there on a platter, why not indulge?

I respect men who are so bluntly honest about their pursuit of the skirts. Derek Jeter, for example, has smashed through some of the top ladies in the world. He doesn't apologize for it, and he didn't marry some woman to paint a picture, then cheat on her with a thousand women and create a scandal. Instead, he offers it at face value.

For the rest, help us ladies out...

What is it you want? The wife or the mistress? The schoolteacher or the stripper? A lady or a freak?

I'm all for people hookin up, and if a pimp is what you're good at being, go get it!! But what I don't understand is the ones who have it all right in front of them and it still just isn't enough.

Many women, by nature, have a need to be needed. We want to provide for, cook for, clean for, and give love to our man. This is where shit gets crazy and wires get crossed.

Men want to be cared for. They love the attention. They want to feel special just as women do. And then, they want to watch the game and see cheerleaders shake their asses.

It's not meant to disrespect us ladies, it's natural to most men. Unfortunately, they don't understand how that makes us feel.

When you are a good woman, and I mean a really good woman, you expect a certain level of respect in relationships. Unfortunately, this is often hard to find.

Ladies, you have to understand, there's four types of men:

Type One loves ass. Period. He wants to see it, wants to get it, and does. It is a sport to him, and even a necessary part of his day. He is not the committing type (although he may someday become it). He is a bona fide Skirt Chaser. Only women seeking a self- esteem boost will hook up with this dude, only to find it takes a hit when he doesn't choose them.

Type Two loves ass, but is realistic. He may or may not get significant amount of ass, but he can find a level of commitment in a relationship. He still will be mesmerized by ass, and any woman with him will have to understand that he will window shop like a motherfucker but will not go into the store. Women with strong self-esteem can work with this guy, but self- doubt can be explosive in this relationship.

Type Three has the least interest in ass. By this, I mean, he is still a man, still will watch porn, still won't turn away from a hot beezy, but his Twitter and Facebook isn't filled with strippers and porn stars. He's the man most women want, even if they've chosen type One or Two as a mate instead. Women of all self-esteem levels can handle this guy.

Type Four is gay. It's not relevant to what women want, because we can't have him anyway. PS, he's typically the prettiest and has the best taste in everything from clothing to shoes to vacation destinations.

Having stated the above, it's now your job, ladies, to choose accordingly. Be realistic with yourselves. Do you really want the Type One? He's got charisma. He has a bright, sparkly Colgate smile and developed chest and shoulder muscles. He has the car. He also has a phone that rings a lot. He also has plans right after your date is over—and they're with another woman.

Type Two will charm you, and you may fall for him. But when you're on the phone with him, he will sometimes lose focus on your conversation as he scans through pictures of other half naked (or completely naked) women. Can you handle it? Can you reassure yourself that he still chooses you?

Type Three is who I recommend for most of us, and really, is the best pick. If you want to feel like the most beautiful woman in the world, which most of us do, this guy will make this happen for you. He would close up Maxim if you walked into the room in sexy lingerie. (I don't say sweats, because…well, let's be real here). But you get the picture.

The bottom line is, don't settle for less than what you really want, and can handle. It's up to you to set the value for yourself and draw the line where it's best drawn for you. Stop harboring unrealistic expectations for men. Stop getting pissed at him for being who he was the day you met him. And, for fucks sake, stop letting your self-esteem be negatively impacted by something you set yourself up for. It's like Katt Williams said,

''Bitch it's called SELF-ESTEEM! It's esteem of your mothafuckin' self. How am I gonna fuck up how you feel about youuuuuu, simple bitch?''

The Emperor Has No Clothes

I know I just got done speaking on self- esteem, but I'm sorry...I'm just not done.

Every day I talk to friends, read peoples' blogs, watch my twitter timeline, and watch completely wonderful people--not just ladies--get passed by, talking about their frustration in love and rejection, and hear stories of how they were overlooked or just plain dissed by some other person.

So many people buy into this ridiculous pressure from society to be perfect and to seek perfection.

We also are told to keep seeking bigger, better, shinier, richer, flashier, and just plain upgrade on a constant basis. Unfortunately, people have taken this theory and translated it to love.

They now get a girlfriend/boyfriend, and instead of choosing someone and committing, they choose someone and continue shopping for an upgraded model. Or, they don't choose at all--they hit the pause button, tie someone up (figuratively) and continue the search.

This can really fuck up the other person's self-esteem, *if they put up with the shit*

The biggest irony in all this, to me, is that someone with such low self-esteem they feel a need to prove to themselves they can get more/better/bigger/badder/etc will hold someone else down in an effort to pursue some kind of enhanced sense of self.

Stop letting other people determine YOUR self worth.

Don't tolerate it. Don't believe the hype. The emperor has no clothes.

Don't be plan B. Don't be just an option or consideration. If you're not "the" choice, you need to be offering yourself up to someone else. Don't think for a moment they'll "grow out of this phase" or "realize eventually" that you're the one. Don't you believe you're worth what you're giving?

Don't let this negatively impact how you view yourself, either. If he/she has to seek attention or the sexual interaction with other people, they clearly have needs one person can't fill, so why invest your energy and time in them?

So many of my friends allow the person they like or love to make them feel "less than". Men get upset because their girl is actively flirting hard with other men to gain their attention. My girl friends are upset because their man is chatting it up with porn stars and half-naked wannabes on Twitter.

Stop trying to compete with the underlings. Those men who chase another man's girl and those women who are #twitterafterdark-ing every man on their timeline are seeking the attention to gain self-worth. And the dumb ones are chasing after it, falling right into the game. If yours is one of the dumb ones, don't fight the current...you'll never win the battle, much less the war.

And if you have the full package in front of you, no one says you are obligated to take it. Some people know what they want, and some people have a need to order the sampler platter. I assure you, that same package you don't want won't go to waste--it will be incredibly cherished by someone else. Right now, while you are exploring all the options and looking in every direction, several someones at a distance is staring at each option you're merely glancing at, and they're envisioning a seige.

If reading that last statement made you feel territorial, you need to check yourself. You have been duped into believing that more is better. Like Confucius says, "Man who chases two rabbits catches neither." Don't be surprised if you end up empty handed at some point.

For the rest of you who are allowing yourself to be "considered" (or tested out, test-driven, in probation periods, or being second string or Junior Varsity) just stop. Don't draw a line, don't give an ultimatum. Just go. Why settle? Somewhere, someone you might want more is out there. Go find them.

Stop looking for perfection. Stop seeking the fantasy. Find what is real and still amazing. Find what is genuine.

The emperor has no clothes, you guys....

Real love is perfect in its imperfection.

Deer Diary

I can count three loves that, even though they've floated out the window, out into oblivion, and I've made my peace with, still bring a mischievous smile to my face.

I suppose I'm blessed for it.

I still am unconvinced that there's a difference between love and infatuation. The two combined bring passion, and isn't that the best part of love? It's what makes you forgive, go back, cry and apologize, fix it, stand by them in a rough time...they found that valuable real estate in your heart and camped out. And even if they leave, it's like they leave the space delightfully haunted.

I'm good at letting people go, pulling a Houdini, or just absolutely doing the ninja move and they're stuck wondering what happened and I'm gone without a trace. It doesn't mean I don't take a piece of them with me.

I had a dream the other night of the love I had right after high school. He was leaving for college across the country, and we had the kind of summer love I know I'll never find again--and wouldn't try to outdo. We were inseparable, did everything together, and ached so much we thought we'd die when he got on the plane for Massachusetts. We were young and thought time lasted forever and all night phone calls turned into emails, then a few cards and letters, and finally we just quietly faded into two different lives.

I woke up from the dream thinking about how it shaped my future relationships. That relationship is far more special to me than the wasted six years I spent with my other ex. And I learned that sometimes you experience something exquisite and you accept it as-is and let it go back to wherever it came from, thankful that you just got to see it at all.

It's like going camping and waking up to see a deer in the woods outside the tent, just hanging out, and you stop and stare, not wanting to move and scare it off, but wanting it to stay as long as possible. You're awestruck by its presence, and when it leaves, you're glad you got to experience it, and you return to the camping trip.

And there's always the hunters that are out just to pick off deer. And those hunters are the reason some deer never go near the campgrounds in the first place. There's also the overzealous people who try to chase the deer or get a picture, and just end up scaring it off. It takes a special unexplainable connection to get the deer to come closer or even most rare--to eat from your hand.

Those star-struck, passionate loves are like seeing that deer. When it's all over, you both return to whatever the path you were on, go your separate ways, and just take that little smile and the piece of that split-second your heart stopped beating and just enjoyed one of the pretties nature has to offer in life.
Meeeeeow.

Dextrocardia

Situs inversus.

It's a condition where your organs are located on the opposite side they should be on. Situs inversus with dextrocardia is even more rare--it is when the heart is situated on the right side of the thorax.

Anyone who's seen Ninja Assassin knows what I'm talking about.

I've recently diagnosed someone special to me with this condition. I noticed it most recently after a period of time when the armor came out, a battle ensued, and shots were fired.

After the dust settled, I found myself (graciously and mercifully!!!) defeated.

While there was still injury, he sustained like a true badass. I know he is a G when it comes to this stuff, but somehow he defeated the odds and left me awestruck.

Shots that would typically slam straight to the heart went clear in, but he remained only mildly scathed...damn you dextrocardia--his heart is on the right side.

It is difficult to withstand the trials and tests of love. Every relationship has its challenges. It's the nature of that fat little bastard that flies around with the darts shooting people. I still am not convinced that Cupid and The Angel of Death are not the same person. But I'm getting closer to believing they are indeed separate beings.

I think it would take a man with this condition to sustain long enough to get to experience the best of what I have to offer. The ability to take some shots that an ordinary man would succumb to, and still stare me straight in the face, refusing to let the shots I've taken be the ones to forge his demise.

On the flip side, however, I realize that this condition is not to be taken for granted. There is still a heart pumping in his chest, and shots fired too many times can still cause a bleed out. Or, they can miss and end up on the right side of the thorax, becoming the makings of a mortal wound.

Today I look back over the elements of battle that brought us to the place we are at today. And looking at what he has triumphed over and what he has withstood to this point, I feel compelled to make myself stop and recognize that an ally stands before me, not the enemy.

As such, he must be treated like an ally. And this means refusing to fire in a direction that may even accidentally cross his path.

I know that because he stood his ground while facing the worst of me, he deserves the best of me.

Grandmaster, I lower my head and bow in honor of your courage strength, and perseverance. Your heart is a thing of beauty, and I recognize that it is in the right place.

Taking A Personal Day

Are things no longer ugly, but just straight fugly in your relationship?

When talking with friends and suggesting ways to fix things, I'm not a big fan of creating space to create closeness, but in some cases, it's like I see both sides, and my best recommendation is a brief "vacation". NOT a breakup, not a weekend to fuck other people.

A 48 hour period of time to revisit yourself because if you don't know who you are, what you're about, and what you really want, how can you be a functioning "half" of a team??

Love is like fire. It can easily consume you, burn you, destroy you, or warm you. And what are the three elements of fire? Fuel, heat, and oxygen. Smokey the Bear taught me that shit. Think of heat as passion. Passion is one of the most beautiful parts of a relationship, and it's what warms you. Fuel is the emotional attachment to the relationship. The friendship that keeps you from leaving or intentionally hurting the other person. It's the core of the fire, because otherwise you'd just be having sex with someone, not be in a relationship.

The last element is oxygen. Air. Breath. Space.

Have you ever been in bed and pressed up to someone so close you have to turn away to inhale some cool, clean air? It's like that in your relationship. If you're figuratively smashed up against that person, you are absolutely going to suffocate your relationship. You each have to be a whole person individually to present something of value to the relationship.

When a flame is about to extinguish, sometimes just a quick blast of oxygen will bring it back to life. The same thing happens when a relationship is smothered. Add a layer of trust issues, last weekend's fight, the responsibilities of life, and even the classic "Seven Year Itch" feeling when you just get restless, and the fire and your relationship can be easily put in danger.

The only way this works is by both people openly communicating the intent, and it doesn't really work if you live together, unless one of you goes away for the weekend. But texts are a no-no. Unfollow each other on twitter. No calls. Straight up 48 hours without each other.

Chances are, you'll meet yourself again, which is always a plus. You also will see the good things you miss about the other person. The little things you take for granted. And in that process, you'll be re-introduced to the relationship.

I don't recommend this for everyone, and I don't think ignoring/running from relationship problems solve everything. But when you're ready to bust out the fire extinguisher and just be done, sometimes it's because you haven't really thought long and hard enough.

Duck Eggs

Two months ago, my kids were playing outside my mother's house and noticed a duck hiding out under a Camellia in the front yard. Upon further investigation,
they saw that she, who we would later name Camille, had built a nest filled with eggs.

For weeks, we would say hello to Camille every time we were at my mom's, and instead of quacking at us, she grew comfortable enough for us to see her without guarding her eggs.

ast month, about the time we anticipated baby duckies to be tagging along behind their mother in an organized little line, my mom found Camille dying on the front lawn, having been attacked by an unknown animal. By her injuries, there would be no chance to save her.

In shock, but feeling a connection to Camille, I decided to try to save her eggs. Upon gathering them, we counted fourteen tiny little duckie souls who now had no ''mommy Animal ''rescues'' and ''wildlife preservationists'' were of no assistance…without live ducks, they didn't care to step in.

This wouldn't work for me. Camille had worked so hard and become part of our family, I wasn't about to let her babies just die. I reached out to twitter for advice/help, and found so many willing to send me information. I set up a home incubator, studied vigorously online to find techniques to nurture eggs until hatching, and went to work.

I learned so much in the process, named all the eggs, and became so excited to think even one egg--just one-- might survive.

Two weeks went by, and slowly, one by one, eggs bled out, stopped developing, and died off. The last day, there were two eggs left: Huey and Dewey.

I had so much faith that all my efforts, as well as Camille's, had not been in vain. So many friends were excited to see even one little baby. I just knew it would work out.

That evening, while scanning the eggs, I actually felt a piece of my heart shatter as I saw that the last two had not survived and had bled out.

All my love, focus, devotion, and most of all, blind faith, had been given for nothing.

Relationships can be like this.

You can believe the stories floating around of people who made it and found it. Stories of hardships, ups and downs, and challenges overcome, but love always prevails. You can hear all your friends say they're so glad you're stepping in and trying it out, and they even share your smiles.

You can, while lying on your bed in the middle of the night, think of what might be to come at some point. You may even carry that love with you throughout the day in everything you do.

While burying the eggs in the yard, I remember trying to figure out what lesson God could possibly have been trying to teach me, particularly because I already am a person of such lack of trust in things and I'm so guarded.

I felt like everything was in vain and that it was a huge waste of my time.

And, in love, I've been dissed by fate like this before.

It's the nature of my personality to want an answer, dammit. I want to KNOW. I want the why's the how's, the details. I want someone to have to look me in the face and say ''I am selfish and it's just too damn bad!'', "_____is my fault and I accept it," or even ''I don't f***ing care!''. Anything but quietly disappearing into non-existence.

It's hard to look over all you put in, all it seemed was naturally there to just ''happen'', and not wonder if it happened because you're supposed to be in it. It's hard to look over it all and think it was for nothing. And worst of all, to know all that love was here, now it's gone to wherever it goes when it's over.

The duck eggs were God's way of telling me I can't always have it my way. And, worse, that I won't always get an answer. Sometimes, it's just because.

Just. Because.

You don't question, ask, freak out, expect anyone to fix it, answer, explain, or justify. It just is, well, duck eggs.

Open Mouth, Insert Paw

Once, I had a lover tell me I am like a cat. I might bite unexpectedly, I don't like to be picked up and carried around, and that I'm usually "happiest alone, but in the company of others".

He teased me and said that some cats will cuddle you and then, out of nowhere, bite you softly. It's some animalistic cat thing that's not attacking, it's just them getting too comfortable with humans. At the time, I thought he was an idiot. Time, however, has made me wise. Fairly recently I failed to make time to see the one person I actually give a shit about. (Mr. Grandmaster for those of you who stay current on this blog). He was in town for a week, I had a bunch of work to do and instead of clearing out the schedule (which I should have done), I just let work take up my time until it was almost too late. And talking with a fellow feral cat, who is now domesticated successfully, she pointed out that if I hate living in the wild so much and have a human to be in contact with (especially one I really like), I should stop being a dick, I mean, wild cat, and just go make the time. In fact, she said to go "Pull a Meg Ryan" and stop right where I'm at, turn around, and make my way to him.

I, at the last minute (literally...) called and cancelled several meetings, made a U-Turn at a stoplight, and hauled ass to the airport to at least get to see him and say goodbye.

Seeing him made me remember how much I really do want to spend time with him, and I felt like a dumb bitch on the ride home, as he left on a plane and I returned to my natural habitat.

Texting today, he mentioned how I don't have a lot of time, and I replied explaining how I learned my lesson last time, and that my "busy schedule" was really just subconscious efforts to keep my distance.

Well, being a Feral Cat, I was pretty black and white in my honesty, and he let me know he understood "either way".

Fuck.

FYI, paws do not taste good.

I tried to continue, letting him know I really just am not good at that stuff and that I mostly don't want to assume space in his world or create space in mine for him based on the assumption he wants a lot from me. Then, (thank GOD), stopped myself and just said "I'm rambling." and shut up. (SMH!)

I wish I was as good at relationships as I am at business.

Instead, I got a reply that he understands that, too, and then I scrambled here to spill my stupidity onto a blog.

I hate this part. This is where, as a feral cat, I usually call it a loss, assume the other party thinks I'm a complete dick/lost cause, and I pounce back into the safety of the wild. With my complete vulnerable honesty, I may have done that weird bite thing some cats do when cuddling you and chased off Mr. Grandmaster. If so, it's my own fault and

I can't take it back.

Maybe I really am that weirdo cat LaundryMatt said I was. Maybe I really am just a dick. Or maybe my problem with commitment is me not being a grown up and making time. Whatever the case, of all things, I'm honest, and I guess, for now, that's something I can hold onto proudly.

The First Goodbye

It was February 7, 2008.

Sitting in my kitchen, I started a blog. I wrote a post about my inability to commit. My disbelief in finding "true love". And my overall lack of faith.

Today, one-hundred-and-ten posts have appeared. Fifteen drafts sit in a queue.

You all have shared laughs, sad moments, ridiculous things I've done, and mistakes I've made. You saw me like, you saw me dislike, and, you got to love with me as well.

If you've never heard of the alpha state, it's the stage of brain activity you're in just before you go to sleep and just as you wake up. It's when your mind is quiet and your thoughts can truly be heard.

A short time ago, I learned about this from someone, and it blew my mind because up until recently, I've tried to make every moment of my life as amazing as that magical time between 2 and 5 am, when I always feel dreamy-eyed, open to possibility, and just plain free.

his blog was a product of that state of mind, and has led me to a book that is nearly complete, a lot of closer friendships, and a ridiculous amount of connection to the art of writing.

On the other hand, the point of the blog started with my commitment phobia and lack of belief in love.

Today, I post this entry to say, with every single tiny bit of me, thank you. Thank you for being part of this journey with me.

While this is the most surreal blog post I've ever written, I'm ready to step out of the alpha state and back to reality.

I've never found it so hard to just find the words I'm trying to say and embellish the page with thousands of little letters finding an artful arrangement that completely lucidly projects my emotions as I am tonight.

But I do know this: I have found love.

I found it and, unfortunately, it's just like I imagined it would be when I started my blog: impossible, inconvenient, painful, difficult to just wear like a new skin. It is also indescribable and consuming.

I no longer have commitment phobia, but I also no longer have even a tangible memento of the love. I don't know if I ever really even "had" it as much as I simply felt it.

That love is like the deer I spoke about in "Deer Diary". It was a beautiful thing that brought some kind of magic into my life for the short period of time it was here. I absolutely don't regret it, and I'm glad to have experienced it. I'd do it all over again.

Cash In Your Chips!!

I think everyone can agree, there is no place like a casino. I mean that in a good way as much as I mean that in a bad way.

And I sat today, hitting the buttons on my little machine I had so scientifically chosen (aka, the one that seemed to just call my name), and I watched as my credits climbed up, then slowly disappeared, then climbed back up...the whole time hearing the sounds of my machine blending in with all the machines in the room.

I listened to people a few sections over shouting "WOO!!" when they hit a small jackpot, and watched other quiet, lonely people sitting in front of their machines, seemingly underwhelmed, yet still hitting buttons like they, themselves, were machines.

And then I realized that the casino is a lot like love.

No worries, I'll elaborate.

See, if the casino is love, the machines are potential lovers . Some you just pass by, some you stop to check out, and some, you sit down and invest in. Sometimes you hit a jackpot right away. Sometimes, you invest in a machine and keep giving and giving until you're out of money. And some people, not the majority, but some lucky ones, really hit it big.

Now, before I continue, I am not discussing gold digging, so dick riding pickpockets, kindly skidaddle. I'm talking about love, not money, as the jackpot.

Really think about it. Think of yourself, and think of the people you know and their personality in love compared to their personality with a slot machine.

I, personally, am one to sit down, and play the "Three Spins and I'm Ghost" game. I sit. I spin that dial three times. If I don't get some kind of a sound from the machine and some credits, I'm out. On to the next. Occasionally, I'll really get an instinctive feeling about a machine and I'll hang out for a while. I've had a select few times where I've continued to pull twenties out of my purse and jam them in the machine, only to be frustrated and out of money. This is so metaphorical when it comes to my love life.

I have a friend who will pick a machine and absolutely stick with it. You couldn't pull her away to save her life. She has chosen a machine, and come hell, high water, or the dreaded "4cents left on the nickel machine", she is do-or-die. Of course, in her love life, she's the same. She will choose a man and absolutely go through hell with/for/because of him and never think to get up and find another machine, no matter how many people are hitting jackpots around her.

I stared back at my machine and really thought about how hard it is to hit "Max Bet". I thought about how deliciously stressful it is to throw a huge chunk of all you brought with you towards a bet that may bring you all kinds of lights and bells and sounds of clinking coins or credits going crazy, or, just....silence. While all the machines around you are going crazy.

Same thing for love.

It's so incredibly hard to shove out a big piece of yourself and leave it to a spin. A chance. You can look at the machine's payouts...you can even have someone next to you tell you how just an hour ago, he saw a guy win $11,000. It still guarantees nothing.

One of the hardest things in love, and at the casino, is watching what you have slowly disappear, and deciding whether to keep hitting buttons or cash out. Do you keep hitting "Max Bet" or do you hold back and start only giving 18 credits?? We all know, giving less credits means you get less back.

I watched sad faced people walk out of
the casino. You could tell they'd lost. And other people stood at the cashier line, giddy with excitement fr om a big win.
I stared back at my machine again, and thought about what my Dad would tell me about gambling. Gambling is strictly for fun.

That's it. If you really want to get a reward, be smart, and invest your money.

So I decided that maybe I need to stop looking at love as a gamble.

It's not win or a loss. Maybe I should stop deciding to
only throw out 18 credits because I'm scared of losing everything. I
definitely should stop staring at a machine and wonder if it's gonna be
something I want to hug and kiss or kick the shit out of at the end of my
time at the casino.

Why? Well, because there's no method to the madness of the casino,
nor is there one in love. How do you *know* it's time to cash in your
chips?? What is too far in, when do you walk away? And when do you
just walk the fuck out of the casino?

Maybe it's time to realize that love is actually an investment.
It's real estate. It's a diversified portfolio. It's a structured
dichotomy of assets and liabilities. It's a privilege and a
responsibility.

You have to put in time, effort, research, and money and be smart
about what you're putting it into. And a strategic, intelligent, grown
up approach to investing beats a quick pull of a lever to let a
machine decide your fate.

Because anyone who knows anything about gambling knows, there
may jackpots, walls of photos of winners with big fat checks, and
stories people tell about a friend of a friend who won big...but in the
end, *the house always wins*.

Note: Shoutout to my Dad for teaching me all the right stuff and
calling my ass out on the wrong stuff. Grazie papa!

jenburger

There's Never A Right Time To Say Goodbye.

There Is A Right Way.

"If love be rough with you, be rough with love. Prick love for pricking and you beat love down." -Mercutio, (Shakespeare's Romeo & Juliet)

Love and respect go hand in hand. Sometimes in the confusion of love and war, which sometimes feel like the same thing, we forget what brought us there in the first place. We let our head rule our hearts.

It's like PTSD for soldiers. Before they deploy, they may be sweet and loving. But after seeing the ugliest parts of war, if you run up quickly to hug them, they may mistake it for an attack, and attack back.

I have been an asshole in my life many, many times. It's rare that I act like a bona fide bitch to someone I love, but it happens. I can coach my friends so well in the classy, peaceful way to have a disagreement with their man or end a relationship, but when it comes to me, I brace for battle and charge ahead.

So if for some reason the person whose heart I was a bit careless with reads this, maybe it will bring a little light to the situation. I was hurt far worse. Because I hurt you and hurt myself in the process. And following suit, you hurt me.

I hope the apology extended is of some kind of comfort to you.

I owed you as much love when you were done as I offered when you weren't.

Love and Basketball

Each side of the court is the same, and every court is supposed to have precisely the same measurements, lines, and boundaries. And the rules, theoretically, should be set.

In love, however, the closest thing to a ref is the voice in your head. It may make the right calls, and it may make all the wrong ones.

Fast breaks can lead to air balls, personal fouls, and even a travel if you're not careful. And unfortunately, in love, you have to play all the positions on your side...not everyone is a good point guard, center, or forward. But you have to be.

I'm great at blocks, and when I'm deep enough in the game, my alley oops and assists are untouchable.

But in basketball, and in love, there's rebounds, lane violations, blocks, and, of course, rejections.

If you're too over-confident in the fast break, you can easily find your ass out of bounds. And of course, there's the penalty involved.

In love, and in basketball, you can't score if you don't cross the mid-court line. In basketball, you have to do this. Unfortunately, in love, playing offense is sometimes being overzealous, and sometimes the other side will play defense. Either way, you are now in their territory, and this means the only thing you'll know is what the other team shows you.

This is where shit gets tricky...you can't just go back. In love, backcourt violations can cost you a lot...sometimes the whole game.

There's time restrictions in love and in basketball. You can't just stand there, ball in hand, and refuse to make a move. If you can't handle it, you need to just pass. If you're in it to win it, you have to just go for a goal.

I charge and I block more than I should. And unfortunately, I'm good for the occasional technical foul.

The only thing I assure you is that being a franchise player will give you a pass or two should this shit go down in the game of love. But if you're a free agent, and you cross the lines, go out of bounds, or end up with too many fouls, the other team may get the free-throws and you can end up at the end of the game sitting on the sidelines with a towel over your head and a shitty cup of Gatorade in your hand instead of a bottle of champagne in the locker room.

For me, I'm a sharp, aggressive player if it's a game, but **I'**d rather be a game played for the love of the game. That's when I'm an MVP, All Star Status. I can team player it like a muthaf*%^$!!!

Take a good, long look at the court you're playing on. If you're seeing an opponent that's not playing for the love of the game and is playing for sport, take note, decide what you're there for, and know that sometimes, it's not the right court to be playing on.

The rules of basketball are straightforward. The rules of love are not. Either way, you have to know them if you're going to win. And most of all, you have to know the other team just as well as you know yourself.

PALATE CLEANSER

Everything You See, I Owe To Drag Queens

Once Sophia Loren was quoted as saying

"Everything you see, I owe to spaghetti."

I share this sentiment, but I thank the Ladyboys.

Next to no one can teach you how to be a real lady like a drag queen can. They have carefully observed the most remarkable women, the most notable of styles, and the most feline of mannerisms, and rolled them into one fierce bitch of a persona.

They are a high octane version of the sexiest bitch you know. They are the sexiest housewife from a pinup magazine. They are the sultriest of models. And, they're the "everyone in this room better stop and worship me right fucking now"est woman you ever met.

Men don't look at Faux Kings (women in drag) just as we don't look at the two super hot paid "lesbians" who make out and go home to their boyfriends. Men's attention is typically trumped when *sex* comes into play, while women can be intrigued and captivated by *sexuality*.

We are mystified by the fact that this anatomical *man* standing before

221

us in 6 inch platform sparkling stilettos and the most exquisite mural of MAC is so fucking savagely gorgeous. And why she is able to be the woman we are only when we feel our most sexy and empowered. She is a Tiffany three carat solitaire princess cut diamond ring and so many days of the week we feel like the Zales $699 Mother's Day special.

They can be bitchy, catty, emotional, and fiercely competitive (no pun intended). They can be self-conscious, backstabbing, manipulative, and lovingly generous. And more than anything, they do not need *our* approval as women. In fact, I've known some who will stand toe to toe to a biological woman and show that bitch who is boss.

I admire them most because they look in the mirror every day with a blank canvas and assess all their flaws, masculine traits, imperfections...shit, even *facial stubble*...and still *work that shit out*. They don't give up because they hate their nose or their eyes are too small. They don't say a pair of heels is too tall or a skirt is too uncomfortable and switch to pants and tennis shoes. They'll, above all else, remember to have that ability to laugh at themselves. They tuck away any sense of distraction (pun intended) and, as RuPaul would say, *don't fuck it up*.

I'll tell you this...I have a pair of Chuck Taylors and lots of sweat pants. I like hoodies just as much as the next girl.

But I *love* my five-inch stiletto-heeled hooker boots. I like wearing my button- up blouses at a 2:3 buttoned-to- unbuttoned ratio. On my worst of days, I'll slide on some deep, rich vixen-red lipstick and an extra two coats of mascara and walk with the tallest of postures and the most confident of stares. If I don't feel like the baddest bitch walking into the room, I will tell myself I am just that.

Any Drag Queen will tell you...they take the canvas they've been given and make it the most undeniably femme-fatale depiction of walking sexiness you ever saw. And even in the worst of times, the most elite competition, holding the cheapest wig and rockin a dress that just doesn't make their ass "pop", they *must*, and do, grab that show by the balls and give it all they've got.

So you fucking fierce sexy bitches of Drag, I salute you. To the ones I've met who've told me a better way to part my hair and the best eyeliner technique for my eyes to Petrilude, Josh Source, Ongina, Jujubee, Raven, and Miss Muthafuckin RuPaul Queen Diva Bitch of Them All, thanks. *I won't fuck it up.*

On twitter, my favorites to follow!!

@joshsource @petrilude (Best makeup tips EVER!!)
@ongina@jujuboston @RavenDavid @jessicawild88
@rupaulsdragrace @rupaul

jenburger

BREAKUPS

Butt-Hurt or Heartbroken?

When you learn the difference, you'll know the proper steps
to recovery.

See, some people mix up "getting ass" and "love". And when your
head accidentally drops the wrong envelope in the wrong box, you
mix the two up.

The hurt corresponds with the anatomical part you did business with.
If you got ass, you leave butt-hurt, which is easy to fix. You just,
well, stop. Love, however, is dealing with the heart, and that's a little
more tricky.

Sometimes it's easy to confuse one with the other. Sometimes you
feel a connection and you just need to release it and compose yourself
and think about *what* the connection was...was it just a feeling?
Unexplainable? Can't put your finger on it? It could've been chemistry
(literally) and not much more. Or if you felt incredibly invested and
they, well, don't, I'm sorry to break it to you, but you were just gettin
ass. Categorize this as "ass" and assume you're butt-hurt.

Problem solved. It's just a matter of time.

Now if you went in and found "love" somehow snuck into
the carry-on baggage, you definitely need to enroll yourself
into Hetox/Shetox, divide and conquer (meaning stay the
fuck away and check yourself), and you'll be ok.

Heartbrokenness is harder to recover from than butt-hurtness, but love is always better than just getting ass, so no pain no gain.

Rarely, there's a combination of both, and all I can say is "fake it till you make it". Start with the butt-hurt part, and the heartbreak will fix itself in time.

When it comes down to it, my best advice, which was cosigned by the group of men I watched a boxing match with today (they were gay, but gays will be even more honest with a neutral-gender perspective on love and hooking up), is this:

Figure out, before you sign the papers, if you want a timeshare, lease, or a lease- to-own. And two months into the contract, re-read that contract and remember the terms you agreed to. And if they no longer work, return to the negotiation table. If both sides aren't in agreement, the contract is null and void, and it's time to call your real estate agent and start shopping. Cause in the first few months, I don't care who you are, what they said, or what you did....you're still only butt-hurt. And then stick with the choice, whatever it is.

And that's the way the nookie crumbles.

Adios, Amigo

goodbyes suck. I don't care who you are, how strong you are, how
much you love, or how much you hate.

long, short, drawn out, or quickly initiated in anger. whether you give
a hug or a middle finger.

whether you amicably part ways or just try your with your absolute
everything to grasp at the little bits you can still hold onto, they suck.

the beginning of the end is so complicated. you never know you're in
it until you're too deep to get back out. and you never fix anything by
trying to get out. the next chapter may overlap, and that's even more
awkward, because you're stuck in two worlds: the one that was, and
the one that will be. the whole time you'll be wondering what the
world that "is" is.

I don't know if it's worse to have something end abruptly, or
if it's the worst to watch something grow and change right
before your eyes and not be able to stop it.

whichever the case, tonight, raise a glass, a shot, or middle finger to
someone you said goodbye to in whatever way you did it.

and if you're lost dead-center in a goodbye right now that is dragging
out, know you're not alone. if you're standing in the center and can
see the distance growing, the comfort fading, and the long chats

becoming shorter and shorter, stop and look back. when you look forward again, just proceed as slow as you can and enjoy the little bit you have while you still have it.

Rolling Papers

No, this isn't a weed blog. Sorry to disappoint.

Walking papers are what you give someone when they're
fired/dumped/etc. Rolling papers are what you give them
when you toss em out the front door and they go rolling off the
porch onto the sidewalk.

I've walked out of dates. I've been sitting on the couch at my
boyfriend's house and stood up, walked out, driven home, and been
done with the relationship. Once, I even got up off my couch in the
home I shared with someone and packed a bag and left, calling the
next day to coordinate a move out and payment of the last month's
rent.

Why?

Because, just like my Dad said, I deserve the best. I deserve
someone who will respect me. Who will push me to be my best.
Someone who will support my dreams, help me grow as a person,
and most of all, respect me.

If you are guilty of mutiny on the ship we share, *you gots to go*.
No Mrs. Nicey Nice. You will get rolled. I have had some very
civilized breakups. I have had grown, respectful discussions
ending things, and still am great friends with several "ex's" that it
just wasn't a good fit with.

Bottom line is, I have standards, and they're set because they're the ones I hold myself to. And I figure if I can hold myself to the standard, it's not impossible to be done.

And that's why some and I graciously part ways, some are shown the door, and a select few others get rolling papers.

jenburger

Sometimes Love Knocks You Down

When it seems like you're letting someone go or they are letting you go and it feels like the worst thing in the world is happening, *remember this*:

Before you cared about them,

you cared for someone else and missed them.

And before that person, you cared for someone *else*. And so on.

And before you know it,

you'll meet someone else to care for and this person will be

"the one before".

And then let them go.

Trainwrecks

Everyone's had at least one love that has gone from something majestic and intoxicating to a big pile of shit you don't even want to glance at.

If you haven't, get off my blog. This is for grown folks.

I keep running on a circular track with love. I'm on that long boring-ass NASCAR track that just keeps going in the same freaking circle over and over. All my friends, family, and old loves are in the grandstands watching me make one lap after another

I make pit stops and the men who want to offer me the world stand and offer me "the perfect love" and tell me they see I'm hurt again, and, unfortunately, they're the most amazing pit crew, but not who I want to finish the race with.

I've been with Mr. Right Nows, Mr. Rights that weren't right for me, assholes, thieves, goons, thugs, conceited pricks, and vanilla personalitied dudes.

And the only time my heart is stolen is by the men who are, I suppose, like me. They have flash in the pan passion and as quickly as it strikes, it's over, and something shiny in the distance catches your eye.

The most recent is no doubt onto the next ones to feign interest in, as am I. And, just like the ones before him, his distance, once it's become cold and the conversations are choppy, the extra smiles and cutesie nicknames are gone, and you are too pissed at love to miss them, just makes me push harder to have more calls, more dates, more attention, even if it's only a distraction.

Look, I hate pain as much as anyone else, but it's like the more it hurts, the more I want the knife jammed in harder. If you're gonna poke or jab me, I'm pressing the knife in the skin. "Let's war. No, really. Slice me. I love it."

I want the pain all at once, now. In fact, I'd love to be told "I don't love you at all." or "I hate you". I want to hear it. I almost *need* *to* so I can walk away without feeling anything--bad *or* good.

I need to be numb, like I was before love brought its bitch ass into the picture. That way, I can go about life unaffected by emotion.

I never promised to be a saint on this blog, I promised honesty.
And check it out--you got it.

I know it was bullshit, I know so many of the sweet things said were said for the sake of saying them, or because he felt them at that second, and, like the one before him, I poured my guts out, just as I do on this blog. And looking at it from the outside, as though my friend lived it, I stare at it and see all the partial truths I accepted, the things that were wrong that I just wanted to believe so much I made myself, and, most of all, all the expression of deep emotion I now look at as a selfish opportunistic act of someone who wasn't in love not willing to tell me I shouldn't be in love.

I think this may be the one that finally pushed me over the "sweet, emotional, real, true "destiny" kinda love. I want a business love.

What is a business love? It is this:

It makes sense for us to be together, I definitely am cool with you, you aren't a complete asshole, and I enjoy having sex with you. But If you walk out the door right now, I'll just pick another.

How's *that* for vows?

This trainwreck went from salvageable to a big clusterfuck of emotional frustration, confusion, and one side trying to be nice and the other side reading too much into it all.

Don't bother calling the fire department. This one's a total loss. I'll just rebuild. And then sell.

Night of the Living Dead

Zombies.

Who has two thumbs and hates 'em? This girl.

I got the text that I, somewhere in my subconscious, knew has been coming for a while. The Ghosts of Summer Past clearly has visited last year's ex.

The whole process is similar to the weeks before Valentine's Day, when all the old loves who find themselves suffocating in singlehood suddenly reminisce on old love and dream up magical ways to chase the high again. They begin texting or emailing, subtly trying to test the waters. Summertime comes rearing its warm, romantic head, and everyone loses their fucking senses and starts forgetting the cold chill that comes with fall.

For this guy, It started a while back when someone asked me about him after having seen him--apparently he had "the best things to say about" me (#ShutDown). Then his friend (not mine) texts me, trying to meet up. I decline, and get a reply saying "Oh, you're still not over ____." I assume he's either fishing for my reply, or he's an insensitive asshole who would date a friend's ex. Either way, (#ShutDown).

Then tonight, direct contact from the Zombie himself: "Hey u. Dont delete this. I just wanna talk."

First of all, the "u" privilege has been lost, my friend.

Second, don't tell me what to do. "I just wanna talk" is the post-breakup version of "Let me just put the tip in". I'm no rookie.

Why do people resurface? What is the point??

Showing back up a year later shows that either you *know* you were wrong or you're a masochist, and it also shows that you didn't learn enough to apply a learned lesson in a new relationship.

I'm not a fan of recycling when it comes to love. I feel that there is a window of time in which it's a permanent fucking wrap. For the time together, there's an equal post-breakup statute of limitations to reconcile. Past that, let it go.

My guidelines:

> Under 1 year: 30 Days

> 1 year to 2 years: 60 Days

> 2+ years: 90 Days

> Marriage: Point of no return. If a divorce is finalized....in fact, if your "Separation" involves no longer cohabiting...it's done.

Think of those closed up, dead relationships as zombies. They're stinky, unattractive, and can eat you alive. The last thing I need is some old, worn-out, decaying romance making an effort to creep its way back into my life. And more people should adopt this mentality.

Now I *will* say that this tends to happen a lot. I will not say I'm perfect or that I'm the dopest woman walking the planet, because that's horse shit.

I am not a troll, I have T&A, I'm talented and funny, and I take care of myself pretty well in terms of finances. My downfalls are that I absorb myself in work a lot and I can be really good at shutting people out if they fuck up and/or show signs of weakness, disloyalty, or general flightiness.

But all that said and done, I'd want me back, too. And the funny thing is, every "ex" I've had has, at one point or another, tried to pull the Zombie move on me.

This particular one is a harder one, because it was the first one that danced the fine line of love & like--it was the most I'd felt in a long time, and it lasted just over a year. But Mr. Big Giant Ego dragged out the commitment until I finally dated other people, then the insecurity came out. Commitment demands, followed by controlling tendencies quickly turned into my lack of respect for him, and ultimately, a parting of ways.

Mdudes reading, and my ladies who follow this blog, please, I beg you, don't be a Zombie and don't fall for the Zombie bait.

Regardless of what was once in a relationship you've had, when things go bad, the foundation has been laid and the behavior patterns have been set. You will *never*, and I mean never re-live the honeymoon period you once had. The magic will always be tainted by whatever ended it the first time. I assure you.

I'm going to ignore the contact, because when I googled "How to Kill A Zombie" it gave me all kinds of lists including lighting them on fire and using Egyptian obelisks. Clearly, those are not options. If the situation continues, their recommendation is to focus on the brain. So I'll have no choice but to remind him that his huge ego can keep him warm at night, and his bragadociousness about the ability to get more ass than a park bench now has an opportunity to be proven-- in my absence. "Baby, please!????"

Baby, *pleeease.*

El Fin

You've seen it before at the end of silent films.

"Fin."

The end.

Here are five phrases to watch for. If you see them/hear them/dream of them/hear someone mumble them in their sleep, it's time to break out the First Aid kit if you want to save the relationship.

One. **I'm Scared.**

> If they elaborate with "of, that, or when", you can open the line of discussion and find out what they are afraid of. Then decide if it's a legit fear. If it is, eliminate it or consider salvaging the friendship.

> If they do not elaborate, show them they can trust you with their feelings. If that doesn't work, take your relationship to the ER. Your friendship is in danger.

Two. I don't want this/I want out

Listen. If they're saying this, they've already thought about it
long enough to find the courage to say this to your
face. This is not a cry/freak out/beg for
them to change their mind time. This is a sit down, shut up, and
listen
time. Fighting this will not save
it. Listening might. You're coding right now, though. Just be
calm and prepare yourself for the end.

Three. I don't want to get hurt.

This means they have distrust for you. This may be
your fault, it may be someone else's. You need to
know this: A) Their distrust means they may not tell
you exactly what has given them a warning sign, but I
assure you, something has them feeling you may
betray/hurt/turn on them B) Prying for answers is
going to make them trust you less. This is a time for
assurance. And actions speak a helluva lot louder
than words.

Four. I don't want to hurt you.

I'm gonna be honest. And you're likely not going to like this.
They care enough to not want to see you hurt, but not enough to
make you the numero uno priority in their decision making. They
have already either thought about, come close to, or acted on an
opportunity to do something you wouldn't like. Please note: Just
like the last one, prying and freaking out is going to do no good.
They already have stated their concern. That was probably a huge
step. This is a Code
Blue. Most of these cases cannot be revived.

Five.   Anything involving the word
"Friendship".

Oh, fuck. The F word of love. When this word is spoken in a
relationship or a relationship-in-the-making, as sad as it is to say,
it's a do-or-die situation. They say this word because more than
likely, they're just not feelin you. There *is* a slight possibility that
they like your company so much they don't want it to go away. But
it's not likely. Also, I hate to be the bearer of bad news, but lots of
times, and I mean lots, these

relationships find a delicate balance of tender friendship and
reserved demonstration of emotion, followed by distance
when one or the other is in a romantic relationship. Trust me
on this...I'm the *queen* of these kinds of friendships.

What's most important to remember in these times is communicate,
and be completely honest with yourself. Do you really (really) want
to be with this person?? If they were to become just your friend,
would you love them enough to *make* that friendship work?

If it is the end, and either you mutually agree or one side declares
it, respect the fact that they cared enough and were grown
enough to state it and talk to
you. Every day, people find out there's someone else, find
themselves in a set- up-argument over something random
which causes a break up, or just come
home to an emptied out apartment or just
stop getting replies to texts and voicemails. Preserve the
friendship when it's there. It's one of the best parts of
relationships.

Also, if you're feeling something just 'off" in your relationship and
want to fix it, remember the above phrases and avoid them. They
communicate to your partner that the kayak you two are in is
headed for a waterfall. And they may put on a life
preserver and be prepared to jump out while you're busy trying to
dig for a map.

jenburger

Eternal Sunshine of the Dirty Mind

I have this theory about bad memories. We all have negative memories about something. For me, it's usually heartbreak or something to do with failed relationships. And it seems the more people I talk to, I'm not alone.

When you break up with someone, fall out of love with someone, or if a relationship in general (even a friendship) fails, sometimes it feels like everything around us reminds us of that person or relationship.

A road you used to travel, a restaurant you used to eat at, or even a song that reminds you of them can make you angry, sad, or just filled with regret or loneliness.

I know you can't delete the memories all together, like in the movie, Eternal Sunshine of the Spotless Mind. I do however, have my own theory on these memories. I'm convinced that we can make new memories of those things to replace the old ones. And, with the redirected association, we'll feel joy instead of pain.

For example, my old roommate Amber and I helped her erase memories of the road she and her ex lived on when she first moved in with me by stopping at every gas station along the route and smashing tiny glass stink bombs in the parking lots. Hours later, the doors were still open and people were still turtling up in their shirts before stopping in to buy a soda. Now, driving along that road, that's her first memory...not the ones of the fun and sad times they had together.

244

And to return the favor, Amber helped me with my sad memories one day last summer....

I had a job interview near Olympia. On my way, I had to find a Kinko's to print my resume, as my printer was down. I decided to use the Puyallup one instead of finding one in unfamiliar territory.

On my way out, I passed "the" laundromat where I met LaundryMatt (if you don't know who he is, it's a long story, but basically, it's a trainwreck of a love story and we parted ways for good last summer). Seeing "the" laundromat, it felt like someone poured hot tea all over my chest, then did a kung fu move, ripping my beating heart out of and holding it in front of my face. Rounding the corner and driving past, I felt sad, but did my usual "turn on some music really loud and move on" technique. By the time I was merging onto Highway 512, I had pretty much forgotten all about it...

After my interview, I stopped to see Amber at work, and, fate had me walking in right as she was getting off work. So, we decided to hang at her house for a while. She had to do a quick laundry load, so we ventured over to the local laundromat.

As we pulled in, she began telling me all the fun tales of the ridiculous shit she's seen while at this magical laundromat. As we got out, a lady outside (who neither Amber nor I knew) began telling us about the wagon full of "35 pounds of mildewy clothes" she brought and "forgot to put the damn Clorox in"...she was going to have to do them all over again.

Once inside, I immediately noted a fantastic "thinking chair" which was undoubtedly a high society piece of furniture sometime in the late 60's, but now just had a society of bacteria and other parasitic creatures burrowing in the goldenrod wool upholstery, a "Barb Wire" pinball game featuring a poorly painted Pamela Anderson and a lot of duct tape, and a sign noting that "Due to gas prices, Dryers are now 6 minutes for 25 Cents".

As we waited, careful not to touch any surfaces with our bare hands, we discussed the local attractions, our days at work and home, and general life aspirations, the clothes whipped around in the dryer, and we were soon on our way.

However, nothing could be so simple. The mildew clothes lady stopped us, and what began as a friendly discussion about karaoke at the Barbecue Inn, and how badly we need to attend, quickly morphed into a lengthy discussion about her intentions to fly to Africa next week to share poetry, the man who runs the Shalimar (no, I can't help you, I have no idea wtf she was referring to) who ripped her off, and the guy who opened a bar that's likely in her name...she's going to check next week.

Her life story continued, as she told us that she now lives below the head of the mafia, visits people in prison to share their writing, and her neighbor hacked her cable so Comcast has blackballed her.

As Amber and I nodded and smiled, trying not to burst her bubble, but to get in the car and go home, I thought to myself "I forgot what laundromats are like!!".

Five hours later, sitting in my kitchen, it dawned on me. Amber had helped me create a new memory of laundromats. While she can't (and I wouldn't want her to) erase all my memories of LaundryMatt, I certainly won't get so sappy when I think of dropping my quarters into the machines and wheeled basket races until owners throw you out.

I'll think of mildew clothes lady and the mafia.

FIN

I'd love a storybook ending

...but I'm done.

It's gonna take one slick, smart, inventive, creative, sweet, real, patient man to get past the giant tsunami of a wall that I'm setting up camp behind.

I suppose it's for the best. I guess? Ladies and gentlemen, we are back to
square one. And my give a shit account for love is overdrawn.

#ThatIsAll

7104650R0

Made in the USA
Charleston, SC
21 January 2011